THE LITTLE BOOK
THAT
BUILDS
WEALTH

Little Book Big Profits Series

In the *Little Book Big Profits* series, the brightest icons in the financial world write on topics that range from tried-and-true investment strategies to tomorrow's new trends. Each book offers a unique perspective on investing, allowing the reader to pick and choose from the very best in investment advice today.

Books in the *Little Book Big Profits* series include:

The Little Book That Beats the Market, where Joel Greenblatt, founder and managing partner at Gotham Capital, reveals a "magic formula" that is easy to use and makes buying good companies at bargain prices automatic, enabling you to successfully beat the market and professional managers by a wide margin.

The Little Book of Value Investing, where Christopher Browne, managing director of Tweedy, Browne Company, LLC, the oldest value investing firm on Wall Street, simply and succinctly explains how value investing, one of the most effective investment strategies ever created, works, and shows you how it can be applied globally.

The Little Book of Common Sense Investing, where Vanguard Group founder John C. Bogle shares his own time-tested philosophies, lessons, and personal anecdotes to explain why outperforming the market is an investor illusion, and how the simplest of investment strategies—indexing—can deliver the greatest return to the greatest number of investors.

The Little Book That Makes You Rich, where Louis Navellier, financial analyst and editor of investment newsletters since 1980, offers readers a fundamental understanding of how to get rich using the best in growth investing strategies. Filled with in-depth insights and practical advice, *The Little Book That Makes You Rich* outlines an effective approach to building true wealth in today's markets.

The Little Book That Builds Wealth, where Pat Dorsey, director of stock research for leading independent investment research provider Morningstar, Inc., guides the reader in understanding "economic moats," learning how to measure them against one another, and selecting the best companies for the very best returns.

THE LITTLE BOOK

THAT

BUILDS

WEALTH

The Knockout Formula

for Finding Great Investments

PAT DORSEY

FOREWORD BY JOE MANSUETO
FOUNDER, CHAIRMAN, AND CEO OF MORNINGSTAR, INC.

WILEY

John Wiley & Sons, Inc.

Published by John Wiley & Sons, Inc., Hoboken, New Jersey.
Published simultaneously in Canada.

For general information on our other products and services or for technical support, please contact our Customer Care Department within the United States at (800) 762-2974, outside the United States at (317) 572-3993 or fax (317) 572-4002.

Wiley also publishes its books in a variety of electronic formats. Some content that appears in print may not be available in electronic books. For more information about Wiley products, visit our web site at www.wiley.com.

Library of Congress Cataloging-in-Publication Data:

Dorsey, Pat.
    The little book that builds wealth : Morningstar's knockout formula for finding great investments / Patrick Dorsey.
        p.   cm.—(Little book big profits series)
    Includes index.
    ISBN 978-0-470-22651-3 (cloth)
        1. Investments.   2. Stocks.   3. Investment analysis.   I. Morningstar, Inc.   II. Title.
HG4521.D6463   2008
332.6—dc22

                                                                                2007045591

Printed in the United States of America.

10   9   8   7   6   5   4   3   2   1

Contents

Foreword

—— ❧ ——

WHEN I STARTED Morningstar in 1984, my goal was to help individuals invest in mutual funds. Back then, a few financial publications carried performance data, and that was about it. By providing institutional-quality information at affordable prices, I thought we could meet a growing need.

But I also had another goal. I wanted to build a business with an "economic moat." Warren Buffett coined this term, which refers to the sustainable advantages that protect a company against competitors—the way a moat protects a castle. I discovered Buffett in the early 1980s and studied Berkshire Hathaway's annual reports. There Buffett explains the moat concept, and I thought I could use this insight to help build a business. Economic moats made so much sense to me that the concept is the foundation for our company and for our stock analysis.

I saw a clear market need when I started Morningstar, but I also wanted a business with the potential for a moat. Why spend time, money, and energy only to watch competitors take away our customers?

The business I envisioned would be hard for a competitor to replicate. I wanted Morningstar's economic moat to include a trusted brand, large financial databases, proprietary analytics, a sizable and knowledgeable analyst staff, and a large and loyal customer base. With my background in investing, a growing market need, and a business model that had wide-moat potential, I embarked on my journey.

Over the past 23 years, Morningstar has achieved considerable success. The company now has revenues of more than $400 million, with above-average profitability. We've worked hard to make our moat broader and deeper, and we keep these goals in mind whenever we make new investments in our business.

Moats, however, are also the basis of Morningstar's approach to stock investing. We believe investors should focus their long-term investments on companies with wide economic moats. These companies can earn excess returns for extended periods—above-average gains that should be recognized over time in share prices. There's another plus: You can hold these stocks longer, and that reduces trading costs. So wide-moat companies are great candidates for anyone's core portfolio.

Many people invest by reacting: "My brother-in-law recommended it" or "I read about it in *Money*." It's also easy to get distracted by daily price gyrations and pundits who pontificate about short-term market swings. Far better to a have a conceptual anchor to help you evaluate stocks and build a rational portfolio. That's where moats are invaluable.

While Buffett developed the moat concept, we've taken the idea one step further. We've identified the most common attributes of moats, such as high switching costs and economies of scale, and provided a full analysis of these attributes. Although investing remains an art, we've attempted to make identifying companies with moats more of a science.

Moats are a crucial element in Morningstar's stock ratings. We have more than 100 stock analysts covering 2,000 publicly traded companies across 100 industries. Two main factors determine our ratings: (1) a stock's discount from our estimated fair value, and (2) the size of a company's moat. Each analyst builds a detailed discounted cash flow model to arrive at a company's fair value. The analyst then assigns a moat rating—Wide, Narrow, or None—based on the techniques that you'll learn about in this book. The larger the discount to fair value and the larger the moat, the higher the Morningstar stock rating.

We're seeking companies with moats, but we want to buy them at a significant discount to fair value. This is what the best investors do—legends like Buffett, Bill Nygren at Oakmark Funds, and Mason Hawkins at Longleaf Funds. Morningstar, though, consistently applies this methodology across a broad spectrum of companies.

This broad coverage gives us a unique perspective on the qualities that can give companies a sustainable competitive advantage. Our stock analysts regularly debate moats with their peers and defend their moat ratings to our senior staff. Moats are an important part of the culture at Morningstar and a central theme in our analyst reports.

In this book, Pat Dorsey, who heads up our stock research at Morningstar, takes our collective experience and shares it with you. He gives you an inside look at the thought process we use in evaluating companies at Morningstar.

Pat has been instrumental in the development of our stock research and our economic moat ratings. He is sharp, well-informed, and experienced. We're also fortunate that Pat is a top-notch communicator—both in writing and speaking (you'll often see him on television). As you're about to find out, Pat has a rare ability to explain investing in a clear and entertaining way.

In the pages that follow, Pat explains why we think making investment decisions based on companies' economic moats is such a smart long-term approach—and, most important, how you can use this approach to build wealth over time. You'll learn how to identify companies with moats and gain tools for determining how much a stock is worth, all in a very accessible and engaging way.

Throughout the book, you'll learn about the economic power of moats by studying how specific companies with wide moats have generated above-average profits over many years—whereas businesses lacking moats have often failed to create value for shareholders over time.

Haywood Kelly, our chief of securities analysis, and Catherine Odelbo, president of our Individual Investor business, have also played a central role in developing Morningstar's stock research. Our entire stock analyst staff also deserves much credit for doing high-quality moat analysis on a daily basis.

This book is short. But if you read it carefully, I believe you'll develop a solid foundation for making smart investment decisions. I wish you well in your investments and hope you enjoy our Little Book.

—JOE MANSUETO
FOUNDER, CHAIRMAN, AND CEO, MORNINGSTAR, INC.

Acknowledgments

---~---

ANY BOOK IS A TEAM effort, and this one is no exception.

I am very lucky to work with a group of extremely talented analysts, without whom I would know far less about investing than I do. The contributions of Morningstar's Equity Analyst staff improved this book considerably, especially when it came to making sure I had just the right example to illustrate a particular point. It's a blast to have such sharp colleagues—they make it fun to come in to work every day.

Special thanks go to Haywood Kelly, Morningstar's chief of securities analysis, for valuable editorial feedback—and for hiring me at Morningstar many years ago. I'm also grateful to director of stock analysis Heather Brilliant for quickly and seamlessly shouldering my managerial duties while I completed this book. Last but not least, Chris Cantore turned ideas into graphics, Karen Wallace tightened my prose, and Maureen Dahlen and Sara Mersinger kept the project on track. Thanks to all four.

Credit is also due to Catherine Odelbo, president of securities analysis, for her leadership of Morningstar's equity research efforts, and of course to Morningstar founder Joe Mansueto for building a world-class firm that always puts investors first. Thanks, Joe.

No one, however, deserves more gratitude than my wife Katherine, whose love and support are my most precious assets. Along with little Ben and Alice, our twins, she brings happiness to each day.

THE LITTLE BOOK
THAT
BUILDS
WEALTH

The Game Plan

T HERE ARE LOTS OF WAYS to make money in the stock market. You can play the Wall Street game, keep a sharp eye on trends, and try to guess which companies will beat earnings estimates each quarter, but you'll face quite a lot of competition. You can buy strong stocks with bullish chart patterns or superfast growth, but you'll run the risk that no buyers will emerge to take the shares off your hands at a higher price. You can buy dirt-cheap stocks with little regard for the quality of the underlying business, but you'll have to balance the outsize returns in the stocks that bounce back with the losses in those that fade from existence.

Or you can simply buy wonderful companies at reasonable prices, and let those companies compound cash over long periods of time. Surprisingly, there aren't all that many money managers who follow this strategy, even though it's the one used by some of the world's most successful investors. (Warren Buffett is the best-known.)

The game plan you need to follow to implement this strategy is simple:

1. Identify businesses that can generate above-average profits for many years.
2. Wait until the shares of those businesses trade for less than their intrinsic value, and then buy.
3. Hold those shares until either the business deteriorates, the shares become overvalued, or you find a better investment. This holding period should be measured in years, not months.
4. Repeat as necessary.

This *Little Book* is largely about the first step—finding wonderful businesses with long-term potential. If you can do this, you'll already be ahead of most investors. Later in the book, I'll give you some tips on valuing stocks, as well as some guidance on when you want to sell a stock and move on to the next opportunity.

Why is it so important to find businesses that can crank out high profits for many years? To answer this question, step back and think about the purpose of a company, which is to take investors' money and generate a return on it. Companies are really just big machines that take in capital, invest it in products or services, and either create more capital (good businesses) or spit out less capital than they took in (bad businesses). A company that can generate high returns on its capital for many years will compound wealth at a very prodigious clip.*

Companies that can do this are not common, however, because high returns on capital attract competitors like bees to honey. That's how capitalism works, after all—money seeks the areas of highest expected return, which means that competition quickly arrives at the doorstep of a company with fat profits.

So in general, returns on capital are what we call "mean-reverting." In other words, companies with high returns see them dwindle as competition moves in, and

---

*Return on capital is the best benchmark of a company's profitability. It measures how effectively a company uses all of its assets—factories, people, investments—to make money for shareholders. You might think of it in the same way as the return achieved by the manager of a mutual fund, except that a company's managers invest in projects and products rather than stocks and bonds. More about return on capital in Chapter 2.

companies with low returns see them improve as either they move into new lines of business or their competitors leave the playing field.

But some companies are able to withstand the relentless onslaught of competition for long periods of time, and these are the wealth-compounding machines that can form the bedrock of your portfolio. For example, think about companies like Anheuser-Busch, Oracle, and Johnson & Johnson—they're all extremely profitable and have faced intense competitive threats for many years, yet they still crank out very high returns on capital. Maybe they just got lucky, or (more likely) maybe those firms have some special characteristics that most companies lack.

How can you identify companies like these—ones that not only are great today, but are likely to stay great for many years into the future? You ask a deceptively simple question about the companies in which you plan to invest: "What prevents a smart, well-financed competitor from moving in on this company's turf?"

To answer this question, look for specific structural characteristics called competitive advantages or economic moats. Just as moats around medieval castles kept the opposition at bay, economic moats protect the high returns on capital enjoyed by the world's best companies. If you can identify companies that have moats and you can purchase their shares at reasonable prices, you'll build a portfolio of wonderful businesses that will greatly improve your odds of doing well in the stock market.

So, what is it about moats that makes them so special? That's the subject of Chapter 1. In Chapter 2, I show you how to watch out for false positives—company characteristics that are commonly thought to confer competitive advantage, but actually are not all that reliable. Then we'll spend several chapters digging into the sources of economic moats. These are the traits that endow companies with truly sustainable competitive advantages, so we'll spend a fair amount of time understanding them.

That's the first half of this book. Once we've established a foundation for understanding economic moats, I'll show you how to recognize moats that are eroding, the key role that industry structure plays in creating competitive advantage, and how management can create (and destroy) moats. A chapter of case studies follows that applies competitive analysis to some well-known companies. I'll also give an overview of valuation, because even a wide-moat company will be a poor investment if you pay too much for its shares.

Chapter One

Economic Moats

~

*What's an Economic Moat, and
How Will It Help You Pick
Great Stocks?*

FOR MOST PEOPLE, it's common sense to pay more for something that is more durable. From kitchen appliances to cars to houses, items that will last longer are typically able to command higher prices, because the higher up-front cost will be offset by a few more years of use. Hondas cost more than Kias, contractor-quality tools cost more than those from a corner hardware store, and so forth.

The same concept applies to the stock market. Durable companies—that is, companies that have strong competitive advantages—are more valuable than companies that are at risk of going from hero to zero in a matter of months because they never had much of an advantage over their competition. This is the biggest reason that economic moats should matter to you as an investor: Companies with moats are more valuable than companies without moats. So, if you can identify which companies have economic moats, you'll pay up for only the companies that are really worth it.

To understand why moats increase the value of companies, let's think about what determines the value of a stock. Each share of a company gives the investor a (very) small ownership interest in that firm. Just as an apartment building is worth the present value of the rent that will be paid by its tenants, less maintenance expenses, a company is worth the present value* of the cash we expect it to generate over its lifetime, less whatever the company needs to spend on maintaining and expanding its business.

---

*To calculate present value, we adjust the sum of those future cash flows for their timing and certainty. A dollar in the hand is more valuable than one in the bush, so to speak, and cash we're confident of receiving in the future is worth more than cash flows we're less certain about receiving. I'll go over some basic valuation principles in Chapters 12 and 13, so don't worry if this isn't clear just yet.

So, let's compare two companies, both growing at about the same clip, and both employing about the same amount of capital to generate the same amount of cash. One company has an economic moat, so it should be able to reinvest those cash flows at a high rate of return for a decade or more. The other company does not have a moat, which means that returns on capital will likely plummet as soon as competitors move in.

The company with the moat is worth more today because it will generate economic profits for a longer stretch of time. When you buy shares of the company with the moat, you're buying a stream of cash flows that is protected from competition for many years. It's like paying more for a car that you can drive for a decade versus a clunker that's likely to conk out in a few years.

In Exhibit 1.1, time is on the horizontal axis, and returns on invested capital are on the vertical axis. You can see that returns on capital for the company on the left side—the one with the economic moat—take a long time to slowly slide downward, because the firm is able to keep competitors at bay for a longer time. The no-moat company on the right is subject to much more intense competition, so its returns on capital decline much faster. The dark area is the aggregate economic value generated by each company, and you can see how much larger it is for the company that has a moat.

EXHIBIT 1.1   Company with an Economic Moat versus a Company without a Moat

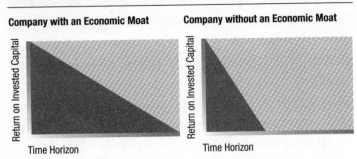

So, a big reason that moats should matter to you as an investor is that they increase the value of companies. Identifying moats will give you a big leg up on picking which companies to buy, and also on deciding what price to pay for them.

Moats Matter for Lots of Reasons

Why else should moats be a core part of your stock-picking process?

Thinking about moats can protect your investment capital in a number of ways. For one thing, it enforces investment discipline, making it less likely that you will overpay for a hot company with a shaky competitive advantage. High returns on capital will *always* be competed away eventually, and for most companies—and their investors—the regression is fast and painful.

Think of all the once-hot teen retailers whose brands are now deader than a hoop skirt, or the fast-growing technology firms whose competitive advantage disappeared overnight when another firm launched a better widget into the market. It's easy to get caught up in fat profit margins and fast growth, but the *duration* of those fat profits is what really matters. Moats give us a framework for separating the here-today-and-gone-tomorrow stocks from the companies with real sticking power.

Also, if you are right about the moat, your odds of permanent capital impairment—that is, irrevocably losing a ton of money on your investment—decline considerably. Companies with moats are more likely to reliably increase their intrinsic value over time, so if you wind up buying their shares at a valuation that (in hindsight) is somewhat high, the growth in intrinsic value will protect your investment returns. Companies without moats are more likely to suffer sharp, sudden decreases in their intrinsic value when they hit competitive speed bumps, and that means you'll want to pay less for their shares.

Companies with moats also have greater resilience, because firms that can fall back on a structural competitive advantage are more likely to recover from temporary troubles. Think about Coca-Cola's disastrous launches of New Coke years ago, and C2 more recently—they were both complete flops that cost the company a lot of money, but because Coca-Cola could fall back on its core brand, neither mistake killed the company.

Coke also was very slow to recognize the shift in consumer preferences toward noncarbonated beverages such as water and juice, and this was a big reason behind the firm's anemic growth over the past several years. But because Coke controls its distribution channel, it managed to recover somewhat by launching Dasani water and pushing other newly acquired noncarbonated brands through that channel.

Or look back to McDonald's troubles in the early part of this decade. Quick-service restaurants are an incredibly competitive business, so you'd think that a firm that let customer service degrade and failed to stay in touch with changing consumer tastes would have been complete toast. And in fact, that's the way the business press largely portrayed Mickey D's in 2002 and 2003. Yet McDonald's iconic brand and massive scale enabled it to retool and bounce back in a way that a no-moat restaurant chain could not have done.

This resiliency of companies with moats is a huge psychological backstop for an investor who is looking to buy wonderful companies at reasonable prices, because high-quality firms become good values only when something goes awry. But if you analyze a company's moat prior to it becoming cheap—that is, before the headlines change from glowing to groaning—you'll have more insight into whether the firm's troubles are temporary or terminal.

Finally, moats can help you define what is called a "circle of competence." Most investors do better if they limit their investing to an area they know well—financial-services firms, for example, or tech stocks—rather than trying to cast too broad a net. Instead of becoming an expert in a set of industries, why not become an expert in firms with competitive advantages, regardless of what business they are in? You'll limit a vast and unworkable investment universe to a smaller one composed of high-quality firms that you can understand well.

You're in luck, because that's exactly what I want to do for you with this book: make you an expert at recognizing economic moats. If you can see moats where others don't, you'll pay bargain prices for the great companies of tomorrow. Of equal importance, if you can recognize no-moat businesses that are being priced in the market as if they have durable competitive advantages, you'll avoid stocks with the potential to damage your portfolio.

The Bottom Line

1. Buying a share of stock means that you own a tiny—okay, *really* tiny—piece of the business.
2. The value of a business is equal to all the cash it will generate in the future.

(continued)

3. A business that can profitably generate cash for a long time is worth more today than a business that may be profitable only for a short time.

4. Return on capital is the best way to judge a company's profitability. It measures how good a company is at taking investors' money and generating a return on it.

5. Economic moats can protect companies from competition, helping them earn more money for a long time, and therefore making them more valuable to an investor.

Chapter Two

Mistaken Moats

~

*Don't Be Fooled by These Illusory
Competitive Advantages.*

THERE'S A COMMON CANARD in investing that runs, "Bet on
the jockey, not on the horse"—the notion is that the quality
of a management team matters more than the quality of a
business. I suppose that in horse racing it makes sense. After
all, racing horses are bred and trained to run fast, and so the
playing field among horses seems relatively level. I may be on
thin ice here, having never actually been to a horse race, but
I think it's fair to say that mules and Shetland ponies don't
race against thoroughbreds.

The business world is different. In the stock market, mules and Shetland ponies *do* race against thoroughbreds, and the best jockey in the world can't do much if his mount is only weeks from being put out to pasture. By contrast, even an inexperienced jockey would likely do better than average riding a horse that had won the Kentucky Derby. As an investor, your job is to focus on the horses, not the jockeys.

Why? Because the single most important thing to remember about moats is that they are structural characteristics of a business that are likely to persist for a number of years, and that would be very hard for a competitor to replicate.

Moats depend less on managerial brilliance—how a company plays the hand it is dealt—than they do on what cards the company holds in the first place. To strain the gambling analogy further, the best poker player in the world with a pair of deuces stands little chance against a rank amateur with a straight flush.

Although there are times when smart strategies can create a competitive advantage in a tough industry (think Dell or Southwest Airlines), the cold, hard fact is that some businesses are structurally just better positioned than others. Even a poorly managed pharmaceutical firm or bank will crank out long-term returns on capital that leave the very best refiner or auto-parts company in the dust. A pig with lipstick is still a pig.

Because Wall Street is typically so focused on short-term results, it's easy to confuse fleeting good news with the characteristics of long-term competitive advantage.

In my experience, the most common "mistaken moats" are *great products, strong market share, great execution, and great management.* These four traps can lure you into thinking that a company has a moat when the odds are good that it actually doesn't.

Moat . . . or Trap?

Great products rarely make a moat, though they can certainly juice short-term results. For example, Chrysler virtually printed money for a few years when it rolled out the first minivan in the 1980s. Of course, in an industry where fat profit margins are tough to come by, this success did not go unnoticed at Chrysler's competitors, all of whom rushed to roll out minivans of their own. No structural characteristic of the automobile market prevented other firms from entering Chrysler's profit pool, so they crashed the minivan party as quickly as possible.

Contrast this experience with that of a small auto-parts supplier named Gentex, which introduced an automatically dimming rearview mirror not too long after Chrysler's minivans arrived on the scene. The auto-parts industry is no less brutal than the market for cars, but Gentex had a slew of patents on its mirrors, which meant that other companies were simply unable to compete with it. The result was fat profit margins for Gentex for many years, and the company is still posting returns on invested capital north of 20 percent more than two decades after its first mirror hit the market.

One more time, with feeling: Unless a company has an economic moat protecting its business, competition will soon arrive on its doorstep and eat away at its profits. Wall Street is littered with the dead husks of companies that went from hero to zero in a heartbeat.

Remember Krispy Kreme? Great doughnuts, but no economic moat—it is very easy for consumers to switch to a different doughnut brand or to pare back their doughnut consumption. (This was a lesson I had to learn the hard way.) Or how about Tommy Hilfiger, whose brands were all the rage for many years? Overzealous distribution tarnished the brand, Tommy clothing wound up on the closeout racks, and the company fell off a financial cliff. And of course, who can forget Pets.com, eToys, and all the other e-commerce web sites that are now just footnotes to the history of the Internet bubble?

More recently, the ethanol craze is an instructive example. A confluence of events in 2006, including high crude oil prices, tight refining capacity, a change in gasoline standards, and a bumper crop of corn (the main input for ethanol), all combined to produce juicy 35 percent operating margins for the most profitable ethanol producers, and solid profitability for almost all producers. Wall Street hyped ethanol as the next big thing, but unfortunately for investors who valued ethanol stocks as if they could sustain high profits, ethanol is a classic no-moat business. It's a commodity industry with no possible competitive advantage (not even scale, since a huge ethanol plant would actually be at a cost *disadvantage* because it would draw corn from a much larger area, driving up input costs, and it would have to process all of its residual output, which consumes a lot of natural gas). So, you can guess what happened next.

A year later, crude prices were still high and refining capacity in the United States was still tight, but corn prices had skyrocketed, refineries had switched over to the new gasoline standard, and lots more ethanol producers had entered the market. As a result, operating margins plunged for all ethanol producers, and they were actually negative for one of the largest producers. *Without an economic moat, a company's financial results can turn on a dime.*

To be fair, it is occasionally possible to take the success of a blockbuster product or service and leverage it into an economic moat. Look at Hansen Natural, which markets the Monster brand of energy drinks that surged onto the market in the early part of this decade. Rather than resting on its laurels, Hansen used Monster's success to secure a long-term distribution agreement with beverage giant Anheuser-Busch, giving it an advantage over competitors in the energy-drink market.

Anyone who wants to compete with Monster now has to overcome Hansen's distribution advantage. Is this impossible to do? Of course not, because Pepsi and Coke have their own distribution networks. But it does help protect Hansen's profit stream by making it harder for the next upstart energy drink to get in front of consumers, and that's the essence of an economic moat.

What about a company that has had years of success, and is now a very large player in its industry? Surely, companies with large market shares must have economic moats, right?

Unfortunately, bigger is not necessarily better when it comes to digging an economic moat. It is very easy to assume that a company with high market share has a sustainable competitive advantage—how else would it have grabbed a big chunk of the market?—but history shows us that leadership can be fleeting in highly competitive markets. Kodak (film), IBM (PCs), Netscape (Internet browsers), General Motors (automobiles), and Corel (word processing software) are only a few of the firms that have discovered this.

In each of these cases, a dominant firm ceded significant market share to one or more challengers because it failed to build—or maintain—a moat around its business.

So, the question to ask is not *whether* a firm has high market share, but rather *how* the firm achieved that share, which will give you insight into how defensible that dominant position will be.

And in some cases, high market share makes very little difference. For example, in the orthopedic-device industry—artificial hips and knees—even the smaller players crank out very solid returns on invested capital, and market shares change glacially. There is relatively little benefit to being big in this market, because orthopedic surgeons typically don't make implant decisions based on price.

Also, switching costs are relatively high because each company's device is implanted in a slightly different fashion, so doctors tend to stick with one company's devices, and these switching costs are the same for all industry players, regardless of size. Finally, technological innovations are incremental, so there is not much benefit to having an outsized research budget.

So, size *can* help a company create a competitive advantage—more on this in Chapter 7—but it is rarely the source of an economic moat by itself. Likewise, high market share is not necessarily a moat.

What about operational efficiency, often labeled as "great execution"? Some companies are praised for being good at blocking and tackling, and experience shows that some companies manage to achieve goals more reliably than competitors do. Isn't running a tight ship a competitive advantage?

Sadly, no—absent some structural competitive advantage, it's not enough to be more efficient than one's competitors. In fact, if a company's success seems to be based on being leaner and meaner than its peers, odds are good that it operates in a very tough and competitive industry in which efficiency is the only way to prosper. Being more efficient than your peers is a fine strategy, but it's not a sustainable competitive advantage unless it is based on some proprietary process that can't be easily copied.

Talented CEOs are fourth in our parade of mistaken moats. A strong management team may very well help a company perform better—and all else equal, you'd certainly rather own a company run by geniuses than one managed by also-rans—but having a smart person at the helm is not a sustainable competitive advantage for a wide variety of reasons. For one thing, the few studies that have been done to try to isolate the effect of managerial decisions show that management's impact on corporate performance is not that large, after controlling for industry and a variety of other factors. This makes sense, given that the practical impact that one person can have on a very large organization is likely not all that large in the majority of cases.

More important, picking great managers is unlikely to be a useful forward-looking endeavor, and our goal in identifying moats is to try to gain some sense of confidence in the sustainability of a company's future performance. Executives come and go, after all, especially in an era in which hiring a superstar CEO can instantly boost a company's market value by billions of dollars. How do we know that the brilliant manager on whom we're hanging our hopes of future outperformance will still be with the company three years down the road? Generally speaking, we don't. (More on management in Chapter 10.)

And finally, I would submit that assessing managerial brilliance is far easier *ex post* than it is *ex ante*—think back for a moment on all the rising stars of the executive firmament who have since fallen to earth. The difference between Cisco Systems CEO John Chambers and Enron's Kenneth Lay is far easier to recognize with the benefit of 20/20 hindsight. This would be why you rarely see lists of "the next decade's great managers" in the business press. Instead, all you see are backward-looking surveys and studies that assume a company's financial or share-price performance is largely attributable to the CEO. Surveys of top corporate managers asking for opinions about their peers suffer from the same bias.

These Moats Are the Real Deal

So, if great products, high market share, efficient operations, and smart executives are all unreliable signs of an economic moat, what should you look for? Here's your list:

- A company can have *intangible assets,* like brands, patents, or regulatory licenses that allow it to sell products or services that can't be matched by competitors.
- The products or services that a company sells may be hard for customers to give up, which creates *customer switching costs* that give the firm pricing power.
- Some lucky companies benefit from *network economics,* which is a very powerful type of economic moat that can lock out competitors for a long time.
- Finally, some companies have *cost advantages,* stemming from process, location, scale, or access to a unique asset, which allow them to offer goods or services at a lower cost than competitors.

In our experience at Morningstar, these four categories cover the vast majority of firms with moats, and using them as a filter will steer you in the right direction. We have thoroughly analyzed the competitive position of thousands of companies across the globe over the past several years, so these four characteristics have been boiled down from a very large data set.

This framework for identifying economic moats differs from a lot of what has been written in the past about competitive advantage. We think some businesses are simply better than others—*better* being defined as "more likely to generate sustainable high returns on capital"—and there are specific things you can look for to help you sort out the better companies from the pack. This is not a message you will hear often when reading books about business or strategy, and the reason for that is simple.

Most people who write about competitive advantage are selling their ideas to corporate managers, and so they focus on generic strategies that any company can pursue to improve or maintain its competitive position. They want their ideas to be applicable to as wide an audience as possible, so the message is typically along the lines of "Any company can become a top performer if it follows these principles/strategies/goals."

This is useful stuff if you are a go-getting corporate executive trying to improve your company's performance. It's also useful if you're trying to sell a book on strategy to these same executives, since a widely applicable set of principles and a positive message will convince more people to buy into your ideas. After all, a blunt listing of the specific characteristics of great businesses is not likely to be popular among managers whose companies don't have those characteristics.

But as investors, we're not stuck trying to make lemons into lemonade, as are the executives trying to shepherd companies through brutally competitive industries. Instead, we can survey the entire investment landscape, look for the companies that demonstrate signs of economic moats, and focus our attention on those promising candidates. If some industries are more structurally attractive than others, we can spend more time investigating them, because our odds of finding companies with economic moats are higher. We can even write off entire swaths of the market if we don't think they have attractive competitive characteristics.

What we need to know, as investors looking for companies with economic moats, is how to recognize a competitive advantage when we see it—regardless of a company's size, age, or industry. Generic principles like "focus on the core" don't cut the mustard, since they can apply to almost any firm. We need specific characteristics that help separate companies with competitive advantages from companies without competitive advantages.

In *Good to Great* (HarperBusiness, 2001), author Jim Collins wrote, "Greatness is not a matter of circumstance." I would respectfully disagree. In my opinion, greatness is largely a matter of circumstance, and it starts with one of these four competitive advantages. If you can identify them, you'll be head and shoulders ahead of most investors in your search for the very best businesses.

The Bottom Line

1. Moats are structural characteristics inherent to a business, and the cold hard truth is that some businesses are simply better than others.
2. Great products, great size, great execution, and great management do not create long-term competitive advantages. They're nice to have, but they're not enough.
3. The four sources of structural competitive advantage are intangible assets, customer switching costs, the network effect, and cost advantages. If you can find a company with solid returns on capital and one of these characteristics, you've likely found a company with a moat.

Chapter Three

Intangible Assets

~

You Can't Pull Them Off A Shelf, But They Sure Are Valuable.

"INTANGIBLE ASSETS" sounds like a grab-bag category for competitive advantage, and in some ways it is. On the surface, brands, patents, and regulatory licenses have little in common. But as economic moats, they all function in essentially the same way—by establishing a unique position in the marketplace. Any company with one of these advantages has a mini-monopoly, allowing it to extract a lot of value from its customers.

The flip side is that moats based on intangible assets may not be as easy to spot as you think. Brands can lose their luster, patents can be challenged, and licenses can be revoked by the same government that granted them. Let's tackle brands first.

Popular Brands Are Profitable Brands, Right?

One of the most common mistakes investors make concerning brands is assuming that a well-known brand endows its owner with a competitive advantage. In fact, nothing could be further from the truth. A brand creates an economic moat only if it increases the consumer's willingness to pay or increases customer captivity. After all, brands cost money to build and sustain, and if that investment doesn't generate a return via some pricing power or repeat business, then it's not creating a competitive advantage.

The next time you are looking at a company with a well-known consumer brand—or one that argues that its brand is valuable within a certain market niche—ask whether the company is able to charge a premium relative to similar competing products. If not, the brand may not be worth very much.

Look at Sony, for example, which certainly has a well-known brand. Now ask yourself whether you would pay more for a DVD player solely because it has the Sony name on it, if you were comparing it to a DVD player with similar features from Philips Electronics or Samsung or Panasonic. Odds are good that you wouldn't—at least most people wouldn't—because features and price generally matter more to consumers when buying electronics than brands do.

Now compare Sony with two companies that sell very different products, jewelry merchant Tiffany & Company and building-products supplier USG Corporation. What these three firms have in common is that they all sell products that are not very different from those sold by their competitors. Take off the Sony label, and its gadgets seem the same as anyone else's. Remove a Tiffany diamond from the blue box, and it looks no different than one sold by Blue Nile or Borsheims. And USG's "Sheetrock"-branded drywall is exactly the same as the drywall sold by its competitors.

Yet Tiffany is able to charge consumers a lot more on average for diamonds with the same specifications as those sold by its competitors, mainly because they come in a pretty blue box. For example, as of this writing, a 1.08-carat, ideal-cut diamond with G color and VS1 clarity mounted in a platinum band sold for $13,900 from Tiffany. A diamond ring of the exact same size, color, and clarity, a similar cut, and a platinum band sold for $8,948 from Blue Nile. (That's an expensive blue box!) USG's story is even more amazing, because unlike Tiffany—which is a luxury brand that would more logically be able to command a premium—USG sells drywall, about the most pedestrian product imaginable. Moreover, USG's wallboard is basically the same as its competitors'. Check out how USG describes Sheetrock:

> . . . fire-resistant gypsum core encased in 100% recycled natural-finish face paper and 100% recycled liner paper on the back side. The face paper is folded around the long edges to reinforce and protect the core, and the ends are square-cut and finished smooth. Long edges of panels are tapered, allowing joints to be reinforced and concealed with a USG Interior Finish System.

Now, compare this with a competitor's description of its wallboard:

> . . . fire-resistant gypsum core that is encased in 100% recycled natural-finish paper on the face side and sturdy liner paper on the back side. The face paper is folded around the long edges to reinforce and protect the core, with the ends being square-cut and finished smooth. Long edges of the panels are tapered, allowing joints to be reinforced and concealed with a joint compound system.

The two descriptions are the same—almost verbatim. But Sheetrock regularly commands a 10 percent to 15 percent price premium because USG markets heavily to the construction trade, and has built up a reputation for durability and strength.

If a company can charge more for the same product than its peers just by selling it under a brand, that brand very likely constitutes a formidable economic moat. Think about Bayer aspirin—it's the same chemical compound as other aspirins, but Bayer can charge almost twice as much as generic aspirin. That's a powerful brand.

Of course, the ability to brand a true commodity product is relatively rare—most brands are attached to differentiated products like Coke, Oreo cookies, or Mercedes-Benz cars. In these cases, the brand is valuable because it reduces a customer's search costs, but it doesn't necessarily give the company pricing power. In other words, you know what a soft drink will taste like if it is labeled "Coke," and you know that a car will be luxurious and durable because it is made by Daimler AG—but Cokes don't cost more then Pepsis, and Mercedes-Benzes don't cost more than BMWs.

Coke and Pepsi cost about the same, but they taste different. The same goes for Oreos and Hydrox cookies. Mercedes-Benz can't charge a premium relative to similar cars, but it works hard to ensure that its products live up to the reputation for quality and durability that the brand conveys. But because producing cars that outlast the competition costs money, it is hard to argue that Mercedes-Benz has a profitability advantage due to its brand.

The big danger in a brand-based economic moat is that if the brand loses its luster, the company will no longer be able to charge a premium price. For example, Kraft used to absolutely dominate the market for shredded cheese until grocery stores introduced private-label products and consumers realized they could get pretty much the same thing—after all, processed cheese is processed cheese—for a lower price.

The bottom line is that brands *can* create durable competitive advantages, but the popularity of the brand matters much less than whether it actually affects consumers' behavior. If consumers will pay more for a product—or purchase it with regularity—solely because of the brand, you have strong evidence of a moat. But there are plenty of well-known brands attached to products and companies that struggle to earn positive economic returns.

Patent Lawyers Drive Nice Cars

Wouldn't it be great to get legal protection completely barring competitors from selling your product? That's what patents do, and while they can be immensely valuable sources of economic moats, they are not always as durable a competitive advantage as you might think.

First, patents have a finite life, and it's a virtual certainty that competition will arrive quickly once a profitable patent expires. (Ask any large pharmaceutical company.)

Legal maneuvering can sometimes extend the life of a patented product, but guessing which team of lawyers will win a patent battle is a game with poor odds—unless you just happen to specialize in intellectual property law, of course.

Patents are also not irrevocable—they can be challenged, and the more profitable the patent is, the more lawyers will be trying to come up with ways to attack it. Many generic drug firms, for example, make challenging Big Pharma's patents a core part of their business. They may succeed with only one challenge in 10, but the payoff for a successful challenge is so high that the challenges keep coming.

In general, it pays to be wary of any firm that relies on a small number of patented products for its profits, as any challenge to those patents will severely harm the company and will probably be very hard to predict. The only time patents constitute a truly sustainable competitive advantage is when the firm has a demonstrated track record of innovation that you're confident can continue, as well as a wide variety of patented products. Think of 3M, which has literally thousands of patents on hundreds of products, or a large pharmaceutical company such as Merck or Eli Lilly. These firms have been cranking out patents for years, and their historical success gives reasonable assurance that currently patented products will eventually be replaced by new patented products.

Brands are much like patents, in that they can often seem like an almost insurmountable competitive advantage. But they are also a textbook illustration of the way in which capital always seeks the area of highest return—that's why they come under attack as frequently as they do. At Morningstar, we typically assign moats only to companies with diverse patent portfolios and innovative track records. Companies whose futures hinge on a single patented product often promise future returns that sound too good to be true—and oftentimes, that's exactly what they are.

A Little Help from the Man

The final category of intangible assets that can create a lasting competitive advantage is regulatory licenses that make it tough—or impossible—for competitors to enter a market. Typically, this advantage is most potent when a company needs regulatory approval to operate in a market but is not subject to economic oversight with regard to how it prices its products. You might think of the contrast between utilities and pharmaceutical companies. Neither can sell its product (power or drugs) to consumers without approval, but the regulators control what the utility can charge, whereas the U.S. Food and Drug Administration has no say over drug prices. It shouldn't come as much of a surprise that drug companies are currently a lot more profitable than utilities.

In short, if you can find a company that can price like a monopoly without being regulated like one, you've probably found a company with a wide economic moat.

The bond-rating industry is a great example of leveraging a regulatory advantage into a near-monopolistic position. In order to provide ratings for bonds issued in the United States, a company has to be granted the designation of "Nationally Recognized Statistical Ratings Organization." So, right away, any potential competitor to the incumbents knows that it will need to undergo an onerous regulatory inspection if it wants to compete in this industry. It should come as no surprise, then, that companies that rate bonds are fantastically profitable. Moody's Investors Service, for instance, sports operating margins north of 50 percent (not a typo), and returns on capital of around 150 percent.

But you don't need to rate bonds to enjoy a strong competitive advantage based on a regulatory approval. Look at the slot machine industry—about as far from the staid business of bonds as you could imagine.

As you might expect, slots are heavily regulated to ensure that the machines don't give casinos any more than the legally mandated advantage, and to keep unscrupulous people from rigging the machines for their personal gain. It's not easy to get approval to manufacture and sell slot machines, and losing this approval can be financially devastating. One of the industry's smaller players, WMS Industries, temporarily lost regulatory approval in 2001 after a software glitch, and it took the firm three years to recover to its preglitch profit level.

Even so, the regulatory barriers are onerous enough that there are only four meaningful players in the slot machine industry in the United States, and there hasn't been a new competitor in many years. You might have expected an upstart to use WMS's troubles as an opportunity to break into the industry, given that selling slots is a very profitable business, but that didn't happen, partly because the regulatory barriers are so high.

Companies that offer higher-education degrees, like Strayer Education or Apollo Group, also need regulatory approvals, called accreditation. There are different levels of accreditation in the United States, and the most valuable one—which makes it easier for students to transfer credits to public universities—is not at all easy to get.

Having accreditation is a huge competitive advantage by itself, because a degree from a nonaccredited school is worth far less to students than one from an accredited school. Moreover, only accredited schools can accept federally subsidized student loans, and because these are a huge source of revenue for most nonelite educational institutions, potential competitors are put at a further disadvantage. Essentially, there is no way to compete with the incumbents in this highly profitable industry without being accredited, and accreditation is given out only grudgingly by the regulatory agencies.

Moody's, the slot machine industry, and the for-profit education industry are all examples of single licenses or approvals giving companies sustainable competitive advantages. But this kind of moat isn't always based on one large license; sometimes a collection of smaller, hard-to-get approvals can dig an equally wide moat.

My favorite example of this is what I call the NIMBY ("not in my backyard") companies, such as waste haulers and aggregate producers. After all, who wants a landfill or stone quarry located in their neighborhood? Almost no one, which means that existing landfills and stone quarries are extremely valuable. As such, getting new ones approved is close to impossible.

Trash and gravel may not sound exciting, but the moat created by scores of mini-approvals is very durable. After all, companies like trash haulers and aggregate firms rely on hundreds of municipal-level approvals that are unlikely to disappear overnight en masse.

What really makes these locally approved landfills and quarries so valuable for companies like Waste Management and Vulcan Materials is that waste and gravel are inherently local businesses. You can't profitably dump trash hundreds of miles from where it is collected, and you can't truck aggregates much farther than 40 or 50 miles from a quarry without pricing yourself out of the market. (Trash is heavy, and gravel is even heavier.) So, local approvals for landfills and quarries create scores of mini-moats in these industries.

Contrast waste and gravel with another industry that has strong NIMBY characteristics—refining. Although there hasn't been a new refinery built in the United States for decades, and local approvals for expansions of existing refineries are pretty tough to come by, the economic situation of a refinery isn't nearly as good as that of a landfill or quarry. The reason is simple: Refined gasoline has a much higher value-to-weight ratio, and it can also be moved very cheaply via pipelines.

So, if a refinery tried to raise prices in a particular area, gasoline from more distant refineries would flow into the locality to take advantage of the higher prices. As a result, while there are regional variations in gasoline pricing, refiners generally can barely eke out high-single-digit to low-teens returns on capital over a cycle, while aggregate producers and waste haulers enjoy much steadier returns on invested capital in the mid to upper teens over many years.

One Moat Down, Three to Go

Although intangible assets may be just that—I can't haul a brand or patent off a shelf and show it to you—they can be extremely valuable as sources of competitive advantage. They key in assessing intangible assets is thinking about how much value they can create for a company, and how long they are likely to last.

A well-known brand that doesn't confer pricing power or promote customer captivity is not a competitive advantage, no matter how familiar people may be with it. And a regulatory approval that doesn't create high returns on capital—think refiners—isn't all that valuable. Finally, a patent portfolio that is too vulnerable to legal challenge, perhaps because it's not diversified, or perhaps because the company has nothing in the pipeline as a follow-up, doesn't constitute much of a moat.

But if you can find a brand that gives pricing power, or a regulatory approval that limits competition, or a company with a diversified set of patents and a solid history of innovation, then the odds are good you've found a company with a moat.

The Bottom Line

1. Popular brands aren't always profitable brands. If a brand doesn't entice consumers to pay more, it may not create a competitive advantage.

(continued)

2. Patents are wonderful to have, but patent lawyers are not poor. Legal challenges are the biggest risk to a patent moat.

3. Regulations can limit competition—isn't it great when the government does something nice for you? The best kind of regulatory moat is one created by a number of small-scale rules, rather than one big rule that could be changed.

Chapter Four

Switching Costs

~

*Sticky Customers Aren't Messy,
They're Golden.*

WHEN WAS THE LAST TIME you changed banks?

Unless you have moved recently, I'll bet the answer is "It's been awhile," and you wouldn't be alone in sticking with your current bank. If you talk to bankers, you'll find that the average turnover rate for deposits is around 15 percent, implying that the average customer keeps his or her account at a bank for six to seven years.

When you think about it, that's a curiously long time. After all, money is the ultimate commodity, and bank accounts don't vary a whole lot in terms of their features. Why don't people switch banks frequently in search of higher interest rates and lower fees? People will drive a couple of miles out of their way to save a nickel per gallon on gasoline, after all, and that's only a buck or two of savings per fill-up. A bank account that doesn't nickel-and-dime you for late fees and such could easily save you a lot more than that cheap out-of-the-way gas station can.

The answer is pretty simple, of course. Switching from the nearby gas station to the cheaper one costs you maybe 5 to 10 minutes extra of time. That's it. Moreover, you know with certainty that is the only cost, because gasoline is gasoline. But switching bank accounts involves filling out some forms at the new bank and probably changing any direct-deposit or bill-paying arrangements you may have made. So, the known cost is definitely more than a few minutes. And then there's the unknown hassle cost that could occur if your current bank delays or mishandles the transfer to your new bank—your paycheck could go into limbo, or your electricity bill might not get paid.

Now, I'm sure that you know why banks are basically licenses to print money. The *average* bank in the United States earns a return on equity of around 15 percent, a level of profitability that is clearly above average for just about any other kind of company. There are lots of reasons for this, but one of the biggest is that bank customers incur a *switching cost* if they want to move from one bank to another. Plainly speaking, moving your bank account is a royal pain, so people don't do it all that often. Banks know this, so they take advantage of their customers' reluctance to leave by giving them a bit less interest and charging them somewhat higher fees than they would if moving a bank account were as easy as driving from one filling station to another.

As you can see, switching costs are a valuable competitive advantage because a company can extract more money out of its customers if those customers are unlikely to move to a competitor. You find switching costs when the benefit of changing from Company A's product to Company B's product is smaller than the cost of doing so.

Unless you use a product yourself—like a bank account—companies that benefit from switching costs can be hard to find because you need to put yourself in the customer's shoes to really understand the balance between costs and benefits. And, like any competitive advantage, switching costs can strengthen or weaken with time.

Let's start with a software company that is probably familiar to you: Intuit, which makes QuickBooks and TurboTax. Intuit has generated returns on capital north of 30 percent for eight years running, and its two flagship products have each retained a more than 75 percent share of their respective markets by successfully keeping the competition—which has included Microsoft more than once—from eating into its core franchises. Like the bank example, this is somewhat surprising on the face of things. Technology changes rapidly, so it doesn't seem likely that Intuit has held off the competition just by having better features in its software, and Microsoft is no slouch when it comes to squashing competitors. The answer lies in switching costs.

Although strategic decisions by Intuit, such as focusing on ease of use and a large menu of software versions to fit different consumers, have definitely helped the company, a big reason that Intuit has held on to the lion's share of the market for these two products is that there are meaningful switching costs for users of QuickBooks and TurboTax.

If you're running a small business and you've already entered all of your company's data into QuickBooks, switching to a competing program will cost you time. That time is valuable, especially to a small business owner who is likely wearing multiple hats at once. Even if a competing program offered a data-import feature, odds are good that the consumer would want to check a lot of the data herself, because that information is the financial lifeblood of her business. So, the cost in time is likely to be quite high.

And in the same way that you run a risk when you change banks that your accounts will get scrambled, a small business owner switching from QuickBooks to a competing program runs the risk of losing track of some important bit of financial data that got misfiled during the transition. If you think an unpaid gas bill from a scrambled checking account is a problem, imagine if a small business owner didn't have enough cash to pay employees because the accounting program never sent out an invoice to a customer.

What about the benefits of switching? Maybe the competition's program is somewhat cheaper, or maybe it has some features that QuickBooks lacks. But basic accounting is about 500 years old (give or take), so it's not terribly likely that a new bookkeeping program could revolutionize the way a small business keeps track of its finances. Weighing both sides, it's hard to see how the benefits of switching could outweigh the costs—which is why Intuit has dominated the market for years, and will likely continue to dominate it.

The same story could be told of Intuit's TurboTax, though arguably the switching costs are somewhat lower because there is less embedded personal data and the tax code changes every year, giving a potential competitor an easier entrée into the market. But a competing product would still need to be significantly easier to use, much cheaper, or more feature-laden to convince people who view taxes as an annual chore to bother learning a new tax-preparation program. Most people hate doing their taxes, so why would they incur the additional cost of time spent learning a new tax-prep program?

Joined at the Hip

Intuit is a classic example of one broad category of switching costs, which you might think of as companies that benefit from tight integration into their clients' businesses. Small companies keep using QuickBooks because it becomes part and parcel of their daily operations, and untangling it from their business to start afresh with a new accounting program would be costly, and possibly risky as well.

This is perhaps the most common type of switching cost, and we see it in a wide variety of companies. Look at Oracle, the giant software company that sells massive database programs that large companies use to store and retrieve huge amounts of data. Because data are rarely of any use in their raw form, Oracle's databases typically need to be connected to other software programs that analyze, present, or manipulate the raw data. (Think about the last item you bought online—the raw data about the product was probably sitting in an Oracle database, but other programs pulled it together to show you the web page from which you made your purchase.)

So, if a company wanted to change from an Oracle database to one sold by a competitor, not only would it need to move all the data seamlessly from the old database to the new one, but it would also have to reattach all the different programs that pull data from Oracle. That's a time-consuming and expensive proposition, not to mention a risky one—the conversion might not work, which might result in a big business disruption. A competing database would have to be phenomenally better (or cheaper) than an Oracle database for a company to choose to pay the massive cost of ripping out its Oracle database and installing another one.

Data processors and securities custodians are in the same camp as Oracle. Companies like Fiserv, Inc. and State Street Corporation do back-office processing for banks and asset managers—they essentially do all of the heavy data crunching and record keeping that keep many banks and asset managers running smoothly. These companies are so tightly integrated with their clients' businesses that they often boast retention rates of 95 percent or better, making substantial portions of their business essentially annuities.

Now imagine the chaos at a bank if its books didn't balance at night, or the disruption at a large wealth-management firm if clients received incorrect asset pricing on their statements. In this case, the risk of switching probably outweighs any monetary or time considerations, given how unhappy customers would be if the back-office processing went awry. No wonder the challenge for firms like these is not making money, but increasing sales, because almost every client is so reluctant to leave its current custodian or processor.

This type of competitive advantage isn't limited to just service and software companies, of course. For example, there is a neat company called Precision Castparts that sells high-tech, superstrong metal components used in jet aircraft engines and power-plant turbines. Think for a minute about the low tolerance for failure in these kinds of products. Steam turbines in power plants can weigh more than 200 tons and spin at 3,000 revolutions per minute—imagine the consequences of a cracked turbine blade. And of course, a jet engine breakdown at 30,000 feet would be, well, really bad.

So, it should come as little surprise that Precision has been selling to some of its customers for more than 30 years, and that its engineers actually work together with customers like General Electric when they design new products. Look at the cost/benefit balance. The only benefit of GE switching to a new supplier would likely be monetary, as long as Precision keeps up its quality standards. So, by dumping Precision for someone else, GE might be able to build turbines and jet engines for less money, which might help it make a larger profit margin when it sells those products.

What about the cost? Well, the explicit cost is meaningful—the new company would need to spend time getting to know GE's products as intimately as Precision already does—but the real cost in this case is risk. Given the incredibly low tolerance for failure on a turbine or jet engine, it doesn't make sense for GE to try to shave the production cost if it increases the risk of product failure. It would take only one high-profile crack-up caused by a metal component failure to seriously damage GE's reputation, after all, which would definitely hurt future sales.

The result is that Precision can earn some pretty fat margins on the components it sells, partly because its customers would need to find a supplier of similar reliability if they wanted to save money by switching. (The company also does a good job controlling costs.) That switching cost, created by years of delivering high-quality parts to its customers, is what gives Precision a competitive advantage.

Switching Costs Are Everywhere

The beautiful thing about switching costs is that they show up in all kinds of industries. Circling back to software, Adobe's moat is also based on switching costs. Its Photoshop and Illustrator programs are taught to budding designers in school, and they're complex enough that switching to another program would mean significant retraining. Another software company, Autodesk, which makes the AutoCAD digital-design software that is used to spec out everything from bridges to buildings, is in an analogous position. Most engineers learn AutoCAD in college, and their future employers have no desire to incur the loss of productivity that would result from retraining them on new software.

Back in financial services, asset managers have switching costs that are somewhat analogous to those of banks. Money that flows into a mutual fund or wealth-management account tends to stay there—we call these sticky assets—and that money generates fees for many years. For example, during the market-timing scandals in the mutual fund world, even when some asset management firms were caught doing blatantly illegal things, most retained enough assets to remain solidly profitable, despite legal costs and investor redemptions.

Although the explicit cost of moving a mutual fund account from Firm A to Firm B is arguably even lower than moving a bank account, most people perceive the benefits as uncertain. They have to convince themselves that the new and less familiar manager will be better than the manager they have been using, which essentially means admitting they made a mistake choosing their current manager in the first place. This is psychologically tough for most people, so assets tend to stay where they are. The switching costs may not be explicitly large, but the benefits of switching are so uncertain that most people take the path of least resistance and just stay where they are.

Over in the energy sector, the mundane business of propane distribution has fairly high switching costs. In many rural parts of the United States, people aren't hooked up to a distribution grid for natural gas, so they get their heat and cooking gas from tanks of propane sited near their houses. Generally speaking, these tanks aren't owned by the customer but rather leased from the company that supplies the propane. So, if a competing propane distributor comes along with a better price and a customer calls up the existing supplier to cancel the service, the current supplier has to swap tanks with the new supplier, which is a big hassle.

Needless to say, people don't switch propane distributors very often, especially because the existing distributor usually charges a fee if you switch to a competitor. This gives the distributors a decent amount of pricing power, and their high returns on capital are financial proof.

In health care, firms that manufacture laboratory equipment often benefit from switching costs. Waters Corporation, for example, makes sophisticated and expensive machines that perform a process called liquid chromatography (LC), which separates compounds into their chemical components for purification and quality control. For example, an LC machine might test water for contaminants or oil for impurities. A firm that wanted to switch from a Waters LC machine to a competitor not only would need to fork out the substantial cost of a new LC machine—in the neighborhood of $50,000 to $100,000—but also would need to retrain a small army of lab technicians to use the new machine, which results in lost time and decreased productivity. Because the LC process requires the constant use of consumables that are extremely profitable for Waters, you can see how these switching costs help Waters achieve remarkable returns on invested capital north of 30 percent.

You'll notice I haven't mentioned many consumer-oriented firms, such as retailers, restaurants, packaged-goods companies, and the like. That's because low switching costs are the main weakness of these kinds of companies. You can walk from one clothing store to another, or choose a different brand of toothpaste at the grocery store, with almost no effort whatsoever. That makes it very hard for retailers and restaurants to create moats around their businesses. Some, like Wal-Mart and Home Depot, can do it through economies of scale, and some, like Coach, can create moats by building strong brands—but in general, consumer-oriented firms often suffer from low switching costs.

Switching costs can be tough to identify because you often need to have a thorough understanding of a customer's experience—which can be hard if you're not the customer. But this type of economic moat can be very powerful and long-lasting, so it's worth taking the time to seek it out. I hope the examples in this chapter have given you some food for thought.

Our third source of competitive advantage is the subject of the next chapter. Although it is arguably a type of switching cost, the network effect is such a unique and potentially powerful economic moat that it deserves a category all its own.

The Bottom Line

1. Companies that make it tough for customers to use a competitors' product or service create switching costs. If customers are less likely to switch, a company can charge more, which helps maintain high returns on capital.
2. Switching costs come in many flavors—tight integration with a customer's business, monetary costs, and retraining costs, to name just a few.
3. Your bank makes a lot of money from switching costs.

Chapter Five

The Network Effect

— ❧ —

*So Powerful, It Gets a Chapter
to Itself.*

I'VE ALWAYS BEEN amazed by those people who seem to have met everyone in creation. You probably know someone like this yourself—think of that friend who effortlessly schmoozes everyone he or she meets and winds up with a Rolodex the size of a bowling ball. These people create huge networks of contacts that make them desirable acquaintances, because the more people they know, the more people they can connect for mutual benefit. Their social value increases as the number of people in their network grows.

Businesses that benefit from the network effect are very similar; that is, the value of their product or service increases with the number of users. This may sound incredibly simple, but it's actually fairly unusual. Think about your favorite restaurant. That business delivers value to you by providing good food at a reasonable price. It likely doesn't matter much to you whether the place is crowded or empty, and in fact, you'd probably prefer it to be not terribly crowded. The value of the service is almost completely independent of how many other people use it.

Now think about some well-known large companies, like the constituents of the Dow Jones Industrial Average, for example. (I've included Exhibit 5.1 of the stocks in the Dow as a refresher.) Exxon Mobil Corporation? A wonderful business, but it makes money by selling energy products for more money than the cost of finding them. More customers are good for Exxon Mobil, but that's not something you think about when you choose which gas station to use. Citigroup? Companies don't use Citi for corporate banking because their peers do—they use Citi because it offers attractive rates on loans. Wal-Mart? It's the same story. The giant retailer's low costs stem in part from its massive size, but people don't shop

EXHIBIT 5.1   Companies in the Dow Jones Industrial Average

Security Name	Industry	Ticker
IBM	Computer Equipment	IBM
Boeing Company	Aerospace & Defense	BA
3M Company	Diversified Manufacturing	MMM
ExxonMobil Corporation	Oil & Gas	XOM
United Technologies	Diversified Manufacturing	UTX
Caterpillar, Inc.	Construction Machinery	CAT
Procter & Gamble	Household & Personal Products	PG
Altria Group, Inc.	Tobacco	MO
American International Group	Insurance	AIG
Johnson & Johnson	Drugs	JNJ
Honeywell International, Inc.	Diversified	HON
American Express Company	Credit Cards	AXP
Coca-Cola Company	Beverage Manufacturing	KO
McDonald's Corporation	Restaurants	MCD
Merck & Co., Inc.	Drugs	MRK
Hewlett-Packard Company	Computer Equipment	HPQ
Dupont El de Nemours & Co.	Chemicals	DD
Citigroup, Inc.	International Banks	C
J.P. Morgan Chase & Co.	International Banks	JPM
Verizon Communications, Inc.	Telecommunication Services	VZ
Wal-Mart Stores, Inc.	Discount Stores	WMT
AT&T, Inc.	Telecommunication Services	T
General Electric Company	Diversified Manufacturing	GE
Alcoa, Inc.	Aluminum	AA
General Motors Corporation	Automakers	GM
Walt Disney Company	Media Conglomerates	DIS
Home Depot, Inc.	Home Supply	HD
Microsoft Corporation	Software	MSFT
Intel Corporation	Semiconductors	INTC
Pfizer, Inc.	Drugs	PFE

at Wal-Mart because other people shop at Wal-Mart—they shop there because stuff is cheap.

Sticking with Dow components, what about American Express? Ah, now we're onto something. The rewards and perks that Amex offers users help it to compete with other credit cards, but if its cards weren't accepted at millions of places where people want to spend money, Amex could offer triple the level of rewards and still have a tiny number of users. That huge network of merchants is what gives Amex a competitive advantage over any other company that may want to start up a new credit card. The more places you can use your Amex card, the more valuable that card becomes to you, which is a big reason behind the company's recent push to get Amex accepted at smaller merchants like convenience stores and gas stations.

Now think about how many large credit card networks there are in the United States. The top four—Visa, MasterCard, Amex, and Discover—account for 85 percent of all spending on credit cards nationwide. That's a huge amount of market concentration, and it illustrates a fundamental reason why the network effect can be an extremely powerful competitive advantage: Network-based businesses tend to create natural monopolies and oligopolies. As economist and academic Brian Arthur has succinctly put it, "Of networks, there will be few."

This makes a lot of sense. If the value of a good or service increases with the number of people using it, then the most valuable network-based products will be the ones that attract the most users, creating a virtuous circle that squeezes out smaller networks and increases the size of dominant networks. And as the dominant networks get bigger, they also get stronger. That sounds like a pretty powerful competitive advantage.

But of course, the very nature of the network effect means that there won't be a very large number of businesses that benefit from it, given the propensity of networks to consolidate around the leader. Let's put this theory to the test in a simple way by looking at the companies in the Dow Jones Industrial Average and seeing which ones benefit from the network effect.

It turns out that only two companies in the Dow derive the bulk of their competitive advantage from the network effect—Amex and Microsoft. We've already talked about Amex's moat, and the way the network effect helps Microsoft is fairly easy to understand as well. Lots of people use Word, Office, and Windows because, well—lots of people use Word, Office, and Windows.

It's hard to argue that Windows is the acme of PC operating systems, but its massive user base means that you pretty much have to know how to operate a Windows-based PC to survive in corporate America. Word and

Excel are similar. Even if a competitor showed up on the scene next week with a word processor or spreadsheet that was five times easier to use and half the price, it would have a hard time gaining traction in the market because Excel and Word have become (like it or not) the common language of knowledge workers around the world.

In fact, there has been an Office competitor called "OpenOffice" on the market for several years, selling for a lot less than Excel and Word—it's actually free, which is a tough price to beat. The word-processing and spreadsheet programs look and feel a lot like Word and Excel, and the files are (largely) compatible with their Microsoft analogs. I've tried OpenOffice, and it's pretty good. But it really hasn't gained much market share among mainstream businesses because there are some small differences, and since the rest of the world still uses Microsoft Office, people don't want to bother using a program that produces files they might not be able to share with others.

If a product that is pretty good and costs nothing can't dent a company's market share, I think you can safely say that company has a competitive advantage.

There is another interesting fact that comes out of our quick tour through the Dow, which is that Amex and Microsoft both operate in relatively new industries. Credit cards have been around for only a few decades, after all, and the PC industry is even younger. As you look for network-based businesses, you'll find this is not a fluke—the network effect is much more common among businesses based on information or knowledge transfer than among businesses based on physical capital.

This is the case because information is what economists call a "nonrival" good. Most goods can be used by only one person at a time—if I buy a big earthmover from Caterpillar, no one else can use it while I'm excavating a foundation. (These types of things are called "rival" goods.) But I can use the Amex payment network at the same time as millions of other cardholders, in the same way that all those cardholders could use the New York Stock Exchange (NYSE) at the same time to find out how much some shares of American Express would cost. One person's use of the Amex network or the NYSE does not impede the ability of others to use those networks—and in fact, the more people who use these networks, the more valuable they are to others.

The bottom line is that you're most likely to find the network effect in businesses based on sharing information, or connecting users together, rather than in businesses that deal in rival (physical) goods. As we'll see later in the chapter, this is not exclusively the case, but it's a good rule of thumb.

By this point, I imagine that you have a good idea of why network effects are such a powerful competitive advantage: A competing firm would need to replicate the network—or at least come close—before users would see more value in the new network and switch away from the existing one. Generally speaking, that's a really tall order. It can happen under the right set of circumstances, as we'll see when we discuss financial exchanges later in the chapter, but network-based businesses are usually pretty durable. To see why, let's take a look at a business that is barely a decade old, but which is already the canonical example of the network effect: eBay.

Networks in Action

Saying that eBay dominates the U.S. online auction market is like saying that Ansel Adams took some decent snapshots of America's national parks. "Dominates" is putting it mildly. As of this writing, eBay had at least an 85 percent share of Internet auction traffic in the United States, and because it is virtually certain that visitors to eBay spend more per transaction and are more likely to buy than are visitors to rival sites, eBay's share of dollars spent in online auctions is likely much higher than 85 percent. The reason why should be obvious after the foregoing discussion of the network effect: The buyers are on eBay because the sellers are there, and vice versa.

Even if a competing site were to launch tomorrow with fees that were a fraction of eBay's, it would be unlikely to get much traffic—no buyers, no sellers, and so forth. And the intrepid first users wouldn't have the benefit of eBay's feedback ratings, telling them which other users they can trust to fulfill a transaction, nor could they be assured of getting the best price, given the paucity of other users. (I once asked a candidate applying for an analyst job at Morningstar what he would do if I played venture capitalist, gave him huge amounts of financial backing, and told him to go beat eBay at its own game in the United States. He thought for a minute and then replied, "I'd return the money." Good answer.)

However, eBay has not been at all successful in some markets, and we can learn a lot about the network effect by briefly examining why this has been the case. In Japan, eBay doesn't even have a presence—Yahoo! Japan has the vast majority of the country's online auction market. The reason here is even simpler than you might think: Yahoo! Japan offered auction services five months before eBay did, and so it was able to amass a large group of buyers and sellers quickly. Further, Yahoo! Japan had the foresight to advertise heavily and to not charge fees initially, both of which helped it to build critical mass faster. By the time eBay launched, Yahoo! Japan had already won—using the same network effect that let eBay dominate the U.S. market. EBay spent a few years trying to compete, but eventually realized that it was beaten, and pulled out of Japan completely.

If eBay's experiences in the United States and in Japan are clear-cut examples of how an early lead can build on itself when network economics are in play, the company's travails in China showed that being first is not always enough—even moats based on the network effect can be overcome under some circumstances. At one point a few years ago, eBay operated the largest online auction site in China, with about a 90 percent share of traffic. However, a home-grown competitor emerged, slashed its listing fees to zero, and introduced some features that were particularly attractive to the Chinese market. EBay lost market share very swiftly, and eventually retreated from the market.

The lesson here is that in a fast-growing market with consumer preferences that are still being formed around a new type of service—online auctions, in this case—the network effect can be subject to successful attack. Of course, eBay's slow response to competitive threats didn't help matters, nor did the fact that its competitor in this case was a Chinese company, and thus gained some advantage from being a local hero of sorts.

But enough about eBay—let's look at some other examples of the network effect in action.

It's not much of a leap to go from eBay, which is really just an online exchange for all kinds of physical goods, to financial markets like the NASDAQ, the New York Stock

Exchange, and the Chicago Mercantile Exchange. Financial exchanges benefit from the network effect much as eBay does, but with some crucial differences that help illuminate when network economics are at their strongest, and when they can break down.

The mechanics of the network effect for a financial exchange are simple: As more buyers and sellers aggregate on an exchange, exchange participants are increasingly able to find the asset they want at the price they want. In financial parlance, more buyers and sellers lead to greater liquidity. This liquidity can be broad, meaning that participants transact in a wide range of assets, and it can be deep, meaning that participants can trade a large volume of assets without affecting the quoted price.

Sounds like a great business, right? Let the network effect work its magic to build a nice pool of liquidity that's both deep and broad, and watch the profits roll in. That's actually not a bad description of futures exchanges like the Chicago Mercantile Exchange (the Merc) and the New York Mercantile Exchange (NYMEX), which are enormously profitable companies with wide moats due to their network-induced liquidity. Unfortunately, the story is a bit more complicated, because exchanges that trade mainly stocks—like the NYSE and NASDAQ—have much weaker competitive advantages, even though they also have deep pools of liquidity.

In fact, stock exchanges have seen falling returns on capital in recent years as competition has moved in, while futures exchanges have maintained very robust profitability. This is because futures contracts are captive to an individual exchange—if I buy a futures contract on the NYMEX or the Merc, I have to sell it there. (The reason for this is complicated, so just trust me.) Futures exchanges can extract a lot more value from market participants, because they exert more control over each transaction.

Stocks, however, can be bought and sold on a wide variety of exchanges, which leads to much greater price competition. A professional investor might buy a thousand shares of IBM on the NYSE, but wind up selling them on any one of a half dozen other exchanges that also trade Big Blue's shares, if one of those other exchanges offers a better price. Because the pool of liquidity in IBM shares is not limited to any one exchange, none of them benefits from the network effect nearly as much as futures exchanges do.

The lesson here is that for a company to benefit from the network effect, it needs to operate a closed network, and when formerly closed networks open up, the network effect can dissipate in a hurry. It's a good question to ask whenever you're evaluating a company that might benefit from network economics: How might that network open up to other participants?

Moving on from exchanges to other industries, we also see the network effect at work in lots of other areas of the market. Money-transfer firm Western Union is just one good example, and the value of its network to users is demonstrated by the fact that even though its network is three times larger than that of its closest competitor, Western Union processes about five times as many transactions. In other words, Western Union gets more business per location—on average—because its users can send money to more places than they could if they used the competition.

This is a common effect of network-based businesses: The benefit of having a larger network is nonlinear, which means that the economic value of the network increases at a faster rate than its absolute size. You can get some sense of this by looking at Exhibit 5.2 and Exhibit 5.3, which compare the number of nodes in a network—analogous to the number of Western Union locations—with the number of connections between those nodes.

It's pretty incredible to see how fast the number of connections grows as you add more nodes. Practically speaking, you easily can see how attractive the economics are. If a network-based business increases its invested capital by, say, 50 percent to expand its number of nodes from 20 to 30, it increases the number of connections by almost 130 percent, from 190 to 435.

EXHIBIT 5.2   A Few More Nodes Equals a Lot More Connections

Nodes	Connections
2	1
3	3
4	6
5	10
10	45
20	190
30	435
40	780
50	1,225

EXHIBIT 5.3   Nodes and Connections

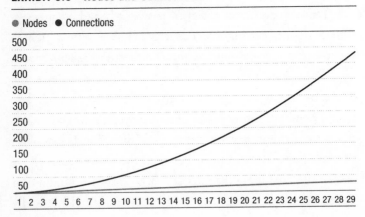

Of course, you need to be a bit careful with this kind of analysis, because the odds are very good that not all connections in a network are equally valuable to all users. Sticking with Western Union as an example, I would imagine that the large number of Western Union branches in various parts of Mexico makes the service very valuable for folks who live in the Pilsen neighborhood in Chicago, where I live, because Pilsen is home to a large number of immigrants with ties to Mexico. But I don't think there are all that many Pilsen residents who are sending money to Dubai or Dhaka, so those particular node-to-node connections aren't as valuable to most folks in Pilsen.

It's fair to say that the value of a network to its users is more closely tied to the number of connections than it is to the number of nodes, but the value-to-connection relationship likely slows down as the number of connections becomes extremely large.

Our next set of network-effect examples comes from an incredibly profitable industry that's not nearly as well known as it should be: third-party logistics. That may sound dull, but 40 percent returns on capital combined with 20 to 30 percent growth rates over more than a decade should pique your interest. How did firms like Expeditors International and C. H. Robinson compile such impressive track records? By building moats based on the network effect.

Both of these companies essentially connect shippers with cargo carriers—think of them as brokers for cargo space. C. H. Robinson operates in the U.S. trucking industry, matching companies with cargo to ship with trucking operators that want to keep their trailers as full as possible. The more shippers with which C. H. Robinson has relationships, the more attractive the company becomes to cargo-hungry truckers, and vice versa. This is a textbook example of the network effect, and it's also a very strong competitive advantage.

Expeditors International is a little bit different. The company operates internationally, and is more than just a matchmaker; essentially, the company's clients ask it to move goods across borders within a defined time frame, and Expeditors takes care of the details. Expeditors buys cargo space on planes and ships on behalf of its clients, fills that space with clients' cargo, and also takes care of whatever other complications—customs, tariffs, warehousing—might arise between the point of origin and the point of departure.

Expeditors International's moat lies in its extensive branch network, which enables it to serve customers more effectively, because no matter where they need to ship stuff, odds are good that Expeditors has a branch at both the sending end and the receiving end. One way to verify this is to do a bit of financial sleuthing. If a larger network really does mean that Expeditors can push more cargo through each branch, then the company's operating income per branch should increase, as new branches add cargo flow to existing ones. It turns out that this is exactly what has happened. (See Exhibit 5.4.)

EXHIBIT 5.4   Expeditors International's Operating Income per Branch ($ Thousands)

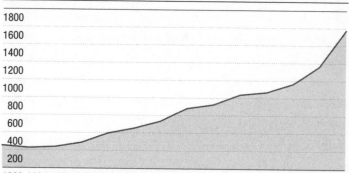

Wrapping up, let's come full circle and look at a company that is a lot like that social butterfly I profiled at the very beginning of the chapter. The Corporate Executive Board publishes best-practices research for large corporations, essentially helping executives figure out how to solve some of the problems they encounter by sharing the experiences of other companies that have faced similar issues. You can see the network effect already—the more companies that are in the Corporate Executive Board's network, the more likely it is to have relevant information for its members. It also helps members by connecting them together for one-off problems.

The beauty of this business is that the published research is actually less valuable than the network at the end of the day.

After all, if you're a time-challenged high-level executive at a large company, which network are you going to join? The one to which all the other time-challenged senior managers from large companies already belong, of course, because they're the people you're competing with, and you probably want to stay abreast of what they're thinking. Any potential competitor to Corporate Executive Board would need to replicate this network to successfully compete with the firm, which seems unlikely as long as its network keeps growing.

As you can see, the network effect is a pretty powerful competitive advantage. It is not insurmountable, but it's a tough one for a competitor to crack in most circumstances. This is one moat that is not easy to find, but it's worth a lot of investigation when you do find it.

The Bottom Line

1. A company benefits from the network effect when the value of its product or service increases with the number of users. Credit cards, online auctions, and some financial exchanges are good examples.

2. The network effect is an extremely powerful type of competitive advantage, and it is most often found in businesses based on sharing information or connecting users together. You don't see it much in businesses that deal in physical goods.

Chapter Six

Cost Advantages

~

*Get Smart, Get Close, or
Be Unique.*

So far, all of the sources of competitive advantage that we've discussed have focused on price, or how much value a company can extract from its customers. Intangible assets, switching costs, and the network effect all allow a company to charge more for a product or service than it would be able to without those advantages. The converse of price, of course, is cost, and companies can also dig moats around their businesses by having sustainable lower costs than the competition.

Cost advantages can sometimes be durable, but they can also disappear very quickly, so as an investor you need to be able to determine whether a company's cost advantage is replicable by a competitor. Lots of companies over the past few years have puffed their chests out about how they lowered costs by moving a call center or manufacturing facility to some low-cost region of the world—China, India, the Philippines, you name it. They act as if management's collective IQ doubled the day some middle manager suggested that the company source low-end parts from a factory with 80 percent lower labor costs.

This is not genius, nor is it a sustainable competitive advantage, because those same low-cost resources are very likely available to any company that wants them. If one auto-parts supplier starts sourcing low-value-added components from China, how long will it take its competitors to make the same phone calls and set up similar supply lines? Not very long at all, because the longer those competitors wait, the more business they are likely to lose as the high-cost producers in a commodity industry. In a globalized economy, using the lowest-cost inputs available is the only way to stay in business for companies operating in price-sensitive industries.

Needless to say, cost advantages matter most in industries where price is a large portion of the customer's purchase criteria. Although these industries are usually characterized as commodity industries, that's not strictly true. Intel, for example, has a massive cost advantage over Advanced Micro Devices (AMD), and microprocessors are not exactly commodities. (Technically, commodities are products with no differentiating factor other than price.)

I think a more useful way to pick out industries in which cost advantages are likely to be a big factor is to imagine whether there are easily available substitutes. Although an Intel chip is certainly different from an AMD chip, they both do pretty much the same thing from a user perspective, and whichever one has the best price-performance ratio is most likely to get the nod from buyers. Intel may have lower long-run costs, but if AMD has chips with much better performance—which has happened for periods of time—users will temporarily switch to its products.

Moving from a really tiny product to a really big one, the story has been largely the same for narrow-body aircraft, believe it or not. Although they are amazingly complex products, a Boeing 737 and an Airbus A320 are not all that different from an airline's perspective—they have similar ranges, carry a similar number of passengers, and so forth. So, an airline shopping for new planes is simply going to see which manufacturer—Boeing or Airbus—will give it the better deal, and make its decision largely on that basis.* (Airlines that use just one type of plane, such as Southwest and JetBlue, are much more the exception than the rule.)

The same can be said of U.S. automakers relative to their Japanese counterparts. No one would confuse a Ford Taurus with a Honda Accord, but they serve pretty much the same function, so the vehicle that costs less (and perhaps breaks down less), is the one that wins in the marketplace. Costs matter a lot to automakers because price is a huge component of the buyer's decision.

Cost advantages can stem from four sources: cheaper processes, better locations, unique assets, and greater scale. Scale-based cost advantages themselves can come in many forms, and they are so important to understand that I devote all of Chapter 7 to helping you understand when bigger really is better. We walk through the other three types of cost advantages in this chapter.

A Better Mousetrap

Process advantages are fascinating because in theory they shouldn't exist for long enough to constitute much of a competitive advantage. After all, if a company figures out a way to deliver a product or service at a lower cost,

---

*The new Boeing 787 may change this dynamic, as it incorporates a number of technological advances that Airbus has not yet been able to match. Older-model jets will still likely be sold mainly on price, though.

wouldn't the logical step for its competitors be to quickly copy that process so they can match the leader's cost structure? This generally does happen eventually, but it can take a lot longer than one might expect. It's worth understanding why that often takes a fair amount of time, during which the originator of the low-cost process can make a lot of money.

I won't beat a very dead horse by going over the process-based cost advantages enjoyed by Dell and low-cost carriers like Southwest Airlines. We've all heard both stories a million times. Dell cut out distributors, sold direct to buyers, and kept inventory very low by building personal computers (PCs) to order. Southwest flew only one type of jet, minimized expensive ground time (fast turns, in airline jargon), and cultivated an employee culture that rewarded thrift.

What's interesting is not as much *how* Dell and Southwest sold PCs and airline seats at far lower costs than the competition, but *why* they were allowed to essentially run away with their respective markets when their low-cost processes were a matter of public record. The answers are different in each case, but they are instructive nonetheless.

In Southwest's case, the incumbent airlines (the majors) didn't copy its low-cost process for a number of reasons. First, a rigid union structure meant that pilots weren't about to start helping clean planes at the incumbents. Second, Southwest's point-to-point route structure would have made it hard for the majors to feed profitable business and international passengers through their expensively maintained hubs. Third, Southwest was an aggressively egalitarian airline—no separate classes, no assigned seats—in an industry that made a lot of money by treating some passengers like royalty and charging them for the privilege. In short, the majors would have had to figuratively blow up their businesses to gain Southwest's cost advantage, and it's hard to blow up your own business.

However, this does not answer why none of the dozens of other upstart airlines succeeded the way Southwest did. Partly, this was because Southwest had already locked up slots at second-tier airports, and partly it was because Southwest had the foresight to lock up a continuous supply of new planes, which have much lower operating costs than used planes. But an equally important reason was that Southwest gained sufficient scale before the majors realized it was much of a threat—and by that time, it was too big to kill. Subsequent start-ups were strangled in their cradles by incumbents that aggressively cut prices on the newcomers' routes, and since the newcomers started with only a few routes, they couldn't withstand the losses for long and folded.

Incumbent PC makers left Dell alone for the same reason that the majors initially gave Southwest a pass: The resellers and retailers that took PCs from the manufacturers to the end user were too vital a link in the distribution chain. IBM or Compaq, or anyone else that would have tried to copy Dell, would have had to blow up its business in order to compete on equal terms. But why didn't other *new* companies copy Dell's business model?

Actually, a couple of other PC companies—Micron and Gateway—did try to copy Dell's business model in the 1990s, but both failed miserably. Micron was too busy trying to run a couple of other business lines to effectively replicate Dell's superefficient supply chain, and Gateway opened retail stores in a bid to differentiate itself and get into the consumer market. It's hard to believe now, but as late as 1996, Dell and Gateway were comparable in size and profitability. Then their paths diverged sharply as Dell cut inventory to unheard-of levels, and Gateway opened stores in strip malls.

Let's look at one more pair of companies with a process-based cost advantage before we try to draw some conclusions. Nucor and Steel Dynamics both operate mini-mills, which—without getting technical—use a process for making steel that is a lot cheaper than the old integrated steel mills run by the likes of U.S. Steel and Bethlehem Steel. Nucor came on the scene in 1969 producing low-grade steel products, and quickly took market share from the integrated mills with lower costs and more flexible production. Steel Dynamics was started in the mid-1990s by Nucor alumni, and is currently the lowest-cost steel producer in the United States—its basic process is the same as Nucor's, but its technology is 25 years newer.

In this example, both Nucor and Steel Dynamics took advantage of a new technology that incumbent operators of integrated mills were unable to implement because they had sunk billions of dollars into their existing operations, which they couldn't just junk to start over. And while other new entrants to the steel market can (and did) start companies with a similar mini-mill process, the old high-cost integrated firms ceded so much market share that Nucor and Steel Dynamics could post respectable returns on capital alongside other new mini-mills.

Now, let's fast-forward all three cases—Southwest, Dell, and the steel mini-mills—to the present. All three are still decent businesses, but their moats are weaker today than they were five or 10 years ago. Why?

Southwest still has a cheaper cost structure than any of the majors—not exactly a hard thing to do, really—but it faces competitors like JetBlue and AirTran that have been able to get access to newer planes and cheap slots at second-tier airports. Also, the declining financial health of the majors made it easier for low-cost airlines to gain scale—the big airlines were struggling so hard to stay afloat that they could not spare the resources to crush upstarts. So, new low-cost carriers have been able to copy important parts of Southwest's secret sauce and match it on cost.

Dell, meanwhile, is still the lowest-cost manufacturer of PCs, but its advantage has shrunk considerably as competitors like Hewlett-Packard have retooled their businesses to cut costs, and high-cost operators like IBM have sold their PC businesses to more savvy owners like Lenovo. Dell has also been hurt by shifts in the PC market. Dell excels at selling cheap desktop PCs to corporations and sophisticated consumers who know exactly what they want, but much of the recent growth in the PC market has come from notebook computers and mass-market consumers. Dell has almost no cost advantage in notebooks, and non-techie consumers are often wary of buying a computer without some handholding from a friendly salesperson at a retail store.

Finally, the mini-mills are facing serious competition from global firms like Arcelor Mittal, which have access to very low-cost steel operations in various corners of the developing world. (Labor costs in Kazakhstan—to name one Arcelor Mittal mill—are pretty darn low.) As trade barriers have declined and new competition with massive scale economies has emerged, the mini-mills' cost advantage has lessened.

The upshot of all these cases is that process-based cost advantages can create a temporary moat if incumbents are unlikely to replicate them immediately, and if new entrants either can't copy the process or doing so is likely to destroy the industry's economics. But notice that the success of two of our examples—Dell and Southwest—was partly based on the inaction (or bad strategy, in Gateway's case) of potential competitors. A moat that is built on lazy or stumbling competitors is not a terribly strong one. So, process-based moats are worth watching closely, because the cost advantage often slips away as competitors either copy the low-cost process or invent one of their own.

Location, Location, Location

A second type of cost advantage stems from having an advantageous location. This type of cost advantage is more durable than one based on process because locations are much harder to duplicate. This advantage occurs most frequently in commodity products that are heavy and cheap—the ratio of value to weight is low—and that are consumed close to where they're produced.

First, let's return to waste haulers and aggregate producers, those pedestrian-but-profitable businesses introduced in Chapter 3. In addition to having regulatory moats, because few communities want a new landfill or gravel quarry in their neighborhood, these types of businesses have a solid location-based cost advantage as well. The further that a garbage truck has to travel to a landfill, or that a dump truck full of gravel has to travel to a construction site, the more it costs to dump the garbage or deliver the gravel. So, companies with landfills and quarries located closer to their customers almost invariably have lower costs, which means competitors have a hard time cracking their markets.

We can look at the quarry-level economics of an aggregate company and see this clearly. Stone, sand, and gravel cost roughly $7 per ton at the quarry site, and an additional $0.10 to $0.15 per ton for every mile spent on the back of a truck getting to the delivery site. So, just five to seven miles of transport increase costs by 10 percent, which is passed on to the customer. In practice, these costs mean that aggregate companies have basically a mini-monopoly on construction customers located fairly close to the quarry, and relatively little competition within the 50-mile radius that is roughly a quarry's addressable market.

Cement plants have similar economics, and similar pricing power within a given cement plant's radius. Ever wonder why you frequently see an old cement plant near a city center or in some other incongruous place? It's because that plant is likely the lowest-cost supplier of cement by far to construction projects in that area, and is probably incredibly profitable—which means it pays a lot of taxes, which helps its owner to fend off local politicians who might want to put up condos on the site. Like quarries, cement plants often create mini-monopolies in their immediate vicinity.

Some—though not all—steel companies also have cheaper costs based on a tough-to-replicate location. For example, formerly state-owned Posco dominates the Korean steel market, controlling an estimated 75 percent of the country's production. Although Posco has to import raw materials, which hurts costs, its location on the same small Korean peninsula as that country's massive automobile and shipbuilding industries gives it an advantage with regard to transportation costs. Also, Posco is located only a day's shipping time from China, which means it can supply Chinese customers at a lower cost than Brazilian or Russian mills with lower input costs but much higher transportation costs. As Chinese steel producers climb up the quality chain and are able to produce larger quantities of high-grade steel, this advantage could erode somewhat, but it has been a powerful one in the recent past.

It's Mine, All Mine

A third type of cost advantage that is generally limited to commodity producers is access to a unique, world-class asset. If a company is lucky enough to own a resource deposit with lower extraction costs than any other comparable resource producer, it can often have a competitive advantage.

Ultra Petroleum, for example, is a midsize energy firm that can produce and sell natural gas at an incredibly low cost due to some advantageous properties in a part of Wyoming. The company locked up land at a very cheap price before its potential was widely recognized, and as a result it is about twice as profitable as the average North American natural-gas producer. For example, most of Ultra's wells cost around $7 million to drill, whereas wells with comparable reserves elsewhere in North America cost other companies in the neighborhood of $17 million to $25 million to drill. That's a massive cost advantage that lets Ultra generate some of the highest returns on capital among the energy companies we cover at Morningstar.

Another firm with this type of cost advantage is an unusual little company that Morningstar has covered for a few years called Compass Minerals, which operates in the truly exciting rock-salt industry. (Think highway deicing, not seasoning french fries.) Compass happens to own a mine in Ontario called Goderich that produces rock salt at some of the lowest costs on the globe due to its unique geology—the vein it is currently mining is more than 100 feet thick—and massive size. Compass also benefits from the Goderich mine's location under Lake Huron, allowing Compass to ship salt into the American Midwest at very low cost along rivers and canals. Because salt is pretty cheap, low transportation costs add to Compass's competitive advantage, and being near a steady source of demand—on average, the Midwest has pretty nasty winter weather—helps as well.

If you look hard enough, you'll find that this type of competitive advantage is not limited to companies that dig stuff out of the ground. Look at Aracruz Cellulose, a Brazilian company that happens to be not only the largest producer of paper pulp in the world, but also the lowest-cost producer. Why? Well, it's pretty easy—the eucalyptus trees that it uses for pulp grow faster in Brazil than anywhere else in the world. (Seedlings mature in about seven years in Brazil, compared with 10 years in neighboring Chile, and 20+ years in temperate climates like North America.) It's not hard to see that if Aracruz's resource base refreshes itself every seven years, while the competition takes 50 to 200 percent longer to grow trees, then Aracruz will be able to produce more pulp with less invested capital than anyone else.

It's Cheap, But Does It Last?

Cost advantages can be extremely powerful sources of competitive advantage, but some are more likely to last a long time than others. Process-based advantages usually bear close watching, because even if they do last for some period of time, it's often because of some temporary limitation on competitors' ability to copy that process. Once that limitation disappears, the moat can get a lot narrower very quickly. Location-based cost advantages and low costs based on ownership of some unique asset are much more durable and easier to hang one's analytical hat on. Companies with location advantages often create mini-monopolies, and world-class natural resource deposits are by definition pretty hard to replicate.

The big kahuna of cost advantages, of course, is scale, and scale advantages can create extremely durable economic moats. When is bigger really better? That's the subject of the next chapter.

The Bottom Line

1. Cost advantages matter most in industries where price is a big part of the customer's purchase decision. Thinking about whether a product or service has an easily available substitute will steer you to industries in which cost advantages can create moats.

2. Cheaper processes, better locations, and unique resources can all create cost advantages—but keep a close eye on process-based advantages. What one company can invent, another can copy.

Chapter Seven

The Size Advantage

~

*Bigger Can Be Better, If You Know
What You're Doing.*

BIGGER IS ONLY relatively better.

When you're thinking about cost advantages that stem from scale, remember one thing: The absolute size of a company matters much less than its size relative to rivals. Two massive firms that dominate an industry—for example, Boeing and Airbus—are unlikely to have meaningful scale-based cost advantages relative to each other. But as we'll discuss further later in this chapter, even a company that is pretty small in absolute terms can have quite a solid moat if it is much larger than its competition.

To understand scale advantages, it's important to remember the difference between fixed and variable costs. If you think about your local grocery store, its fixed costs are rent, utilities, and salaries for some base level of staffing. The variable costs would be the wholesale cost of the merchandise that the store needs to stock the shelves, and perhaps extra compensation costs for high-traffic times of the year like the holidays. A real-estate brokerage office, by contrast, would have almost exclusively variable costs. Aside from an office, a phone, a car, and a computer with a link to the database of homes for sale, an agent doesn't have many costs aside from commissions, which vary with real-estate sales: no sales, no commissions.

Very broadly speaking, the higher the level of fixed costs relative to variable costs, the more consolidated an industry tends to be, because the benefits of size are greater. It's no surprise that there are only a few national package-delivery companies, or automobile manufacturers, or micro-chip producers—but there are thousands of small real-estate agencies, consultancies, law offices, and accounting agencies. A law firm with 1,000 lawyers has no cost advantage over a law firm with 10 lawyers. It may have a greater range of services it can offer, and it may get additional business from that angle, but it is not going to have a meaningful cost advantage over a smaller competitor.

We can break down scale-based cost advantages further into three categories: distribution, manufacturing, and niche markets. Although manufacturing scale tends to get all of the attention in Economics 101, my experience is that the cost advantages stemming from large distribution networks or dominance of a niche market are just as powerful—and, in an increasingly service-oriented economy, they are more common as well.

The Value of the Van

Large distribution networks can be the source of tremendous competitive advantages, and you can easily see why when you think about the economics of moving stuff from point A to point B. Let's look at the fixed and variable costs of running a fleet of delivery trucks. The trucks themselves—whether purchased or leased—are a fixed cost, as are the salaries of their drivers and most of the gasoline that the trucks need to consume as they trundle along their routes. The only real variable costs are overtime wages for busy periods, and some proportion of the gas. (You might think of the fixed fuel cost being what is needed for the truck to complete its normal route, and the variable cost being what's consumed if the truck needs to go to an out-of-the-way location not on the usual route.)

Although building and operating the delivery network is an expensive proposition for a base level of service, the incremental profit on each item that the truck fleet delivers is enormous. Think about it—once the fixed costs are covered, delivering an extra item that is on a delivery route is extremely profitable because the variable cost of making an extra stop is almost nothing. Now imagine that you need to try to compete with a company that has an established distribution network. It has likely covered its fixed costs and is making large incremental profits as it delivers more stuff, while you'll need to take on large losses for a time until (if) you gain enough scale to become profitable.

One of the main reasons, in fact, that United Parcel Service (UPS) has much higher returns on capital than rival FedEx is that it earns a larger proportion of its operating profits from door-to-door delivery of packages, as opposed to overnight letter services. A dense ground delivery network has much better returns on capital than an overnight express service. A delivery van that's only half full will still likely cover its costs, whereas a half-full cargo jet with time-sensitive packages likely will not.

Many businesses with delivery networks can dig this type of economic moat. Consider Darden Restaurants, which operates the Red Lobster chain of casual seafood restaurants in the United States. It may not sound exciting, but getting reasonably fresh seafood to 650 restaurants across an entire continent is not a small task—and having a large distribution network allows Darden to accomplish this more efficiently and at a lower cost than its competitors. With many more restaurants than its closest competitor, Darden clearly benefits from distribution scale.

Moving from tasty crab legs to the less palatable world of medical waste, you can also see a huge distribution advantage in a company called Stericycle, which is the largest company collecting and disposing of medical waste in the United States. Stericycle is 15 times larger than its nearest competitor, giving it unrivaled route density. Having more stops per route leads directly to more profitable routes, higher returns on capital, and a wider economic moat—a large and dense distribution network means that Stericycle can potentially underprice competitors and still generate higher profits.

Large distribution networks are extremely hard to replicate, and are often the source of very wide economic moats. We see this in companies from Sysco, the largest food-service distributor in the United States, to Fastenal, one of the largest U.S. distributors of fastening products for manufacturing firms, to large beverage companies such as Coca-Cola, Pepsi, and Diageo.

Bigger Can Be Better

Cost advantages can also stem from manufacturing scale. The classic example of this is a factory with an assembly line. The closer the factory is to 100 percent capacity, the more profitable it is, and the larger the factory, the easier it is to spread fixed costs like rent and utilities over a larger volume of production. Also, the larger the factory, the easier it is to specialize by individual tasks or to mechanize production. Arguably, the prevalence of this type of cost advantage has diminished somewhat in the recent past as enormous low-cost pools of labor in China and Eastern Europe have become integrated into the global economy, causing some manufacturing to shift away from Europe and North America. Still, it's a very real advantage for some companies.

Perhaps the best example is Exxon Mobil Corporation, which has lower operating costs than any of the other supermajor integrated oil companies by virtue of achieving scale economies in many of its operating segments. Although the scale advantage is less apparent in the company's upstream operations that explore for and extract oil and natural gas, it's very apparent in the firm's refining and chemical operations, which have returns on capital that dwarf those of competitors like Valero and BASF Corporation.

Manufacturing scale needn't be limited to owning a larger production facility than the competition. If we think about scale simply in terms of spreading fixed costs over a larger sales base, we can see that nonmanufacturing companies can also benefit from economies of scale. Video-game giant Electronic Arts, for example, has an easier time creating fantastic video games than smaller companies because the cost of bringing a video game to market—currently around $25 million—is essentially fixed, and Electronic Arts can spread the massive development costs of its video games over a larger overall sales base.

Across the pond in the United Kingdom, we see a similar dynamic at BskyB, the largest provider of pay-television services in that country. Sky can afford to pay far more for content than rivals because it can spread the cost over a larger number of subscribers—it has about three times more subscribers than Virgin Media, its closest competitor. So, Sky can purchase more Premier League football matches, more first-run movies, and more hit U.S. television shows, which attracts more subscribers, which in turn gives Sky the financial muscle to keep beefing up its content offerings. Absent a new market entrant outbidding Sky for a significant chunk of this content and being willing to suffer large financial losses as it tried to poach subscribers, it looks like Sky has a pretty wide economic moat.

Big Fishes in Small Ponds Make Big Money

A final type of scale advantage is domination of a niche market. Even if a company is not big in an absolute sense, being relatively larger than the competition in a specific market segment can confer huge advantages. In fact, companies can build near-monopolies in markets that are only large enough to support one company profitably, because it makes no economic sense for a new entrant to spend the capital necessary to enter the market.

The *Washington Post,* for example, owns a number of cable-TV systems in smaller cities like Boise, Idaho, that are only large enough to support a single cable-service operator. Competitors don't bother spending the capital needed to build a competing system because the profit pool is only large enough for one company. If a competitor did build a second cable system, neither it nor the incumbent would have enough customers to be comfortably profitable. Although the attractive economics of these small-city cable operations have diminished somewhat since satellite television entered the fray, they are still good examples of the niche-market moat.

Companies with niche-market moats can generate fabulous returns on capital while making very mundane products. For example, I doubt that you've ever thought much about industrial pumps, but it turns out that you can make a lot of money manufacturing high-quality paint sprayers and pumps for food processing. A wonderful little firm in Minneapolis called Graco, Inc. makes both, and it generates 40 percent returns on capital in the process.

How is this possible? First, the total market for high-end industrial pumps is not all that large, limiting its attractiveness to large, well-financed competitors. Second, Graco spends liberally—about 3 to 4 percent of sales—on research and development, ensuring that it continually stays at the cutting edge of customers' requirements. Third, Graco's products often deliver results that are highly visible to the end consumer, but represent a small fraction of total production costs. Think of the stain and lacquer on a piece of furniture or the paint job on a new car—the finishing touch is not expensive relative to the product's total cost, but it's the first thing the consumer sees. As a result, Graco can extract premium pricing from customers like furniture manufacturers or automakers. The extra spending doesn't affect the cost of the table or the sports car very much, but it definitely boosts Graco's profit margins.

Although this type of competitive advantage is often found in smaller manufacturing firms, it's not limited to the industrial world. There is a neat little software firm called Blackboard, for example, which has about two-thirds of the market for learning management systems, a type of university-wide software application that connects faculty and students. Blackboard's software allows faculty to post assignments, helps students to collaborate on projects, and enables faculty and students to communicate.

Like industrial pumps, this is not a mammoth market, so it's less likely to attract a giant like Microsoft or Adobe. It is also a highly specialized market, so a competitor would probably need to expend substantial resources to learn what customers want before being successful—and because the market is relatively small, few companies will try.

A final fascinating example of dominating a niche is private infrastructure firms. Although these are not terribly common in the United States, they're becoming more so elsewhere in the world, with airports being perhaps the best example. Many airports around the world are private firms, including most of the airports in Mexico; the Auckland, New Zealand, airport; Schipol in Amsterdam; and several others. While regulatory approval—an intangible asset—is certainly one type of competitive advantage enjoyed by airports, single-competitor economics also apply. Many markets have only enough air traffic to support a single airport profitably, so even if a competitor could get the regulatory approval to open up a second airport near Auckland or Puerto Vallarta, doing so wouldn't necessarily generate attractive returns on capital. This keeps new entrants out of the market, giving many airports very wide economic moats.

The Bottom Line

1. Being a big fish in a small pond is much better than being a bigger fish in a bigger pond. Focus on the fish-to-pond ratio, not the absolute size of the fish.
2. Delivering fish more cheaply than anyone else can be pretty profitable. So can delivering other stuff.
3. Scale economies have nothing to do with the skin on a fish, but they can create durable competitive advantages.

Chapter Eight

Eroding Moats

*I've Lost My Advantage and
I Can't Get Up.*

So far, we've talked almost exclusively about the signs of a strong competitive advantage—the structural characteristics of businesses that create economic moats. Investing would be relatively simple if all we had to do was look for companies with moats, wait for them to trade at reasonable prices, and then lock them away forever to compound capital in competitively advantaged bliss. Sadly, the world is not a static place, which complicates matters considerably.

The best analysis in the world can be rendered moot by unforeseen changes in the competitive landscape. As recently as a decade ago, being a specialist on the New York Stock Exchange was a license to print money. Today, it's like having a monopoly on buggy whips. Thirty years ago, Polaroid was revolutionizing the way people took pictures, but the firm died a slow death long before digital imaging put the final nail in film photography's coffin. Long-distance telephony and newspapers were once reliable and highly profitable businesses, but now they struggle to generate cash. The list goes on and on.

All of these businesses possessed strong competitive advantages at one point in time, but the world changed to their detriment. Although change can be an opportunity, it can also severely erode once-wide economic moats. This is why it is critical to continually monitor the competitive position of the companies in which you have invested, and watch for signs that the moat may be eroding. If you can get an early read on a weakening competitive advantage, you can greatly improve your odds of preserving your gains in a successful investment—or cutting your losses on an unsuccessful one.

Getting Zapped

There are two sides to this threat. The first is the risk that a company that sells technology—software, semiconductors, networking gear, you name it—loses out in the furious race to stay on the cutting edge. Of course, most companies that sell tech products have a hard time building a lasting competitive advantage in the first place, and it's hard to destroy a moat that never existed. Being technologically supplanted by a competitor is simply a fact of life for most technology companies, because they typically win business by having a product that is better/faster/cheaper than their peers' products. So, they constantly run the risk of seeing their competitive advantage disappear in months if a better product hits the market. As one academic who studies competitive advantage has pithily stated, "In the long run, everything is a toaster."

Occasionally, a product is so much better than the rest that its success feeds on itself, and the company becomes the de facto standard for its industry—Research in Motion, purveyor of the ubiquitous BlackBerry mobile e-mail device, might be a good example. But the much more common story for technology vendors without standard-setting power is that they fade into oblivion (remember Palm?) or stumble along for years until a larger firm puts shareholders out of their misery via an acquisition.

Technological disruption is a more unexpected—and severe—threat when it affects nontech companies, because these companies can look like they have very strong competitive advantages before a technological shift permanently hurts their economics. It's one thing to have a competitive advantage destroyed when it barely existed in the first place; it's quite another when a business that once looked like a perpetual cash machine is consigned to irrelevance.

Examples of technological disruption abound. Think about Eastman Kodak, which for decades printed money through its dominance of the U.S. market for photographic film, and which today struggles to find a place in a digital world. From 2002 to 2007, Kodak earned only about $800 million in cumulative operating income, an 85 percent decline from its cumulative operating profits for the previous five years. Whether Kodak can eventually succeed in digital photography is still an open question, but the economics of short product-cycle consumer electronics look tougher than the slow-moving but highly profitable business of selling celluloid, paper, and chemicals that Kodak enjoyed in the past.

Newspapers were once some of the best businesses in the world, reliably throwing off massive cash flows through their lock on local news, advertising, and classifieds. No more—the Internet has done irrevocable damage to the business of distributing daily news. Newspapers aren't about to disappear, but it's unlikely they will ever be as profitable as they once were.

The Internet has also permanently killed long-distance telephony, another business that was once incredibly profitable. Phone companies for decades minted money as the gatekeepers of connectivity between far-flung individuals and businesses. Now that phone calls can be routed over Internet-protocol networks, the legacy telecom carriers face structurally worse economics than they once did. Anyone with a computer and a free piece of software can make calls for pennies per minute, and a once-reliable source of cash for long-distance carriers is now gone forever.

And you can ask any well-coiffed music executive what the Internet has done to the music-publishing business. Ouch.

A final example that should be near and dear to the hearts of investors is the experience of equity exchanges—and especially floor traders and specialists—over the past few decades. Once NASDAQ became a viable competitor by the late 1970s and demonstrated that an all-electronic exchange was a cheaper alternative to a floor-based exchange, Pandora's box was opened. Increasing volume on NASDAQ, combined with ever-lower communications and computing costs, spurred the creation of off-exchange trading networks like Archipelago. The more trading volume that bypassed floor traders and specialists, the more precarious their positions became, with the added headwind of tighter bid-ask spreads hurting profit margins.

Granted, the kind of technological disruption that structurally damages the economics of an entire industry is relatively rare—but it's a painful experience for investors who are unable to recognize the change in time. One thing to remember is that disruptive technologies can hurt the moats of businesses that are *enabled* by technology even more than businesses that *sell* technology, even though investors in technology-enabled firms may not think they own a tech stock.

Industrial Earthquakes

Just as changes in the technological scene can cause once-strong moats to erode, shifts in the structure of industries can also cause lasting damage to companies' competitive advantages. One common change to watch out for is consolidation of a once-fragmented group of customers.

In the United States, the rise of big-box retailers like Target, Wal-Mart, and others has permanently changed the economics of many consumer-products companies for the worse. Although a number of factors have contributed to decreased pricing power for firms like Clorox and Newell Rubbermaid, the increased buying power of a concentrated group of customers certainly tops the list. In Newell's case, the company's brands have also been hurt by Office Max and Staples, which have been pushing private-label office supplies.

In another area of retail, the demise of mom-and-pop hardware stores and their replacement by the Lowe's/

Home Depot duopoly has hurt the economics of many hardware suppliers. Even companies with venerable brands like Stanley Works or Black & Decker have lost pricing power now that they sell a sizable percentage of their wares through Lowe's and Home Depot, which have far more negotiating leverage than a fragmented group of independent hardware stores.

Changes in the industry landscape needn't be local, of course. The entry of low-cost workforces in Eastern Europe, China, and elsewhere into the global labor pool has permanently damaged the economics of many manufacturing businesses. In some cases, the labor differential is so large that companies that may have once benefited from a location-based moat have seen that competitive advantage disappear, as the cost savings from low-cost labor is large enough to offset high transportation costs. The wood-furniture industry in the United States has seen this happen firsthand.

One final change to watch out for is the entry of an irrational competitor into an industry. Companies that are deemed strategic by a national government may take actions that support political or social goals, even though they result in lower profitability. For example, the business of making jet engines for aircraft has been for years a comfortable oligopoly among General Electric, Pratt & Whitney (owned by United Technologies), and UK-based

Rolls-Royce. Standard practice in the industry for a long time has been to sell the engines at or somewhat below cost, and to make money on lucrative service contracts; because jet engines can last for decades, the lengthy stream of service fees can be quite profitable.

But in the mid-1980s, Rolls-Royce ran into some financial difficulties and needed subsidies from the British government to keep the company alive. In order to save jobs and win business at one of the country's highest-profile firms, management began cutting prices on both engines and maintenance contracts. Unfortunately, this practice continued for years after Rolls-Royce returned to consistent profitability, with the result that margins for Pratt and GE suffered for a while, as they were forced to match Rolls' pricing. Jet engines remained a good business with a decent economic moat, and GE's margins in particular have rebounded, but Rolls' actions hurt all three players at the time.

The Bad Kind of Growth

Some kinds of growth can cause moats to erode. In fact, I'd say the single most common self-inflicted wound to competitive advantage occurs when a company pursues growth in areas where it has no moat. Most corporate managers think bigger is always better (in fairness, managers at larger companies tend to get paid more than managers at smaller companies, so it's not illogical in some respects) and so they expand into less profitable businesses.

My favorite example of this is Microsoft. Yes, the company still has a very wide moat, but I'd argue that shareholders in the firm over the past decade have not been well served by the company's attempts to expand outside of its core operating system and office productivity franchises. The list of sinkholes into which Microsoft has poured money is longer than you'd think—the Zune, MSN, and MSNBC are just a start. Did you know that the company once tried to launch a series of kids' toys called Actimates? Or that it blew more than $3 billion on a bunch of European cable companies in the late 1990s?

Although Microsoft would likely be somewhat smaller, in terms of employees and sales, had it never ventured into any of these areas, the company's phenomenal returns on capital would have been even higher without fruitless spending on industries in which the company had no competitive advantage. What business does a software company have starting a *cable news channel*, for goodness' sake?

Like many wide-moat businesses, Microsoft found itself in the enviable position of generating more cash than it needed to reinvest in the core Windows/Office franchises. And—also like more than a few wide-moat businesses—Microsoft chose to take that cash and use it to create and expand businesses in which its competitive advantage was much weaker. Microsoft is so ridiculously profitable that this misuse of cash did not drag overall returns on capital down to an unattractive level, but that's not the case for every company. For less profitable companies, no-moat investments can hurt returns on capital enough to make the entire corporation less attractive as an investment.

You may be asking what Microsoft *should* have done with all that cash flow it didn't need to keep expanding and improving Windows. Well, the company did use some to expand into complementary areas that have succeeded, such as database software and operating systems for servers. It should have just given the rest back to shareholders as a dividend, a vastly underutilized tool for allocating capital efficiently.

A company can fill in its own moat by investing heavily in areas in which it has no competitive advantage.

No, I Won't Pay

This is more of a sign of moat erosion than a cause, but it's important nonetheless. If a company that has regularly been able to raise prices starts getting pushback from customers, you're getting a strong signal that the company's competitive advantage may have weakened.

I'll give you a fairly current example from the analyst team at Morningstar. In late 2006, one of our analysts noticed that Oracle, which sells database software, was less able to raise prices on its software maintenance contracts than it had been in the past. Historically, maintenance contracts have been one of the most lucrative segments of companies that sell huge pieces of software to large businesses. Typically, large corporate customers have favored maintenance done by the original vendor of the software, because that company is presumably the most intimately familiar with the code, and is also the most up-to-date on new versions and features of the software. Also, Oracle would essentially force companies into upgrading by announcing that it would, after a time, no longer support previous versions of the software. So, Oracle raised its maintenance fee a little every year, and customers grumbled a bit but paid anyway.

So why was Oracle getting pushback on maintenance pricing now? We did some digging, and found that a few third-party support companies had sprung up and were getting a decent amount of business. If a third-party company could credibly offer maintenance services, customers wouldn't necessarily have to upgrade to a new version of the software. This seemed like a trend that would likely continue, placing pressure on a highly profitable revenue stream for Oracle, and potentially narrowing its moat.

I've Lost My Moat, and I Can't Get Up

As physicist and philosopher Niels Bohr once said, "Prediction is very difficult, especially if it's about the future." Yet that's exactly what we need to do when assessing the durability of a company's competitive advantage. But sometimes the future throws you a curve ball, and that's when you need to reassess whether a company's moat is still intact or the unexpected turn of events has done permanent damage to the company's competitive advantage.

The Bottom Line

1. Technological change can destroy competitive advantages, but this is a bigger worry for companies that are *enabled* by technology than it is for companies that *sell* technology, because the effects can be more unexpected.

2. If a company's customer base becomes more concentrated, or if a competitor has goals other than making money, the moat may be in danger.

3. Growth is not always good. It's better for a company to make lots of money doing what it is good at, and give the excess back to shareholders, than it is to throw the excess profits at a questionable line of business with no moat. Microsoft could get away with it, but most companies can't.

Chapter Nine

Finding Moats

~

It's a Jungle Out There.

ONE OF THE BEST THINGS about being an intelligent investor is that the world is your oyster. You're not forced to invest in industry A or industry B, so you're free to cast a discerning eye over the entire investment universe, ignoring what you don't like and buying what you do. This freedom is especially important if you are looking to build a portfolio of companies with economic moats, because it's a lot easier to dig a moat in some industries than in others.

Let me repeat myself, because this is a critically important point: Some industries are brutally competitive and have awful economics, and creating a competitive advantage requires the managerial equivalent of a Nobel Prize. Other industries are much less competitive, and even average companies are able to sustain solid returns on capital. (No one ever said life was fair.) As an investor, you'll have better odds hunting for ideas in industries where managers only need to hurdle one-foot bars to succeed than you will looking for long-term winners in industries where the barriers to success are much higher.

Looking at opposite ends of the spectrum, consider auto parts and asset management. No, it's not a fair fight, but that's precisely my point. Morningstar covers 13 auto-parts companies, only two of which have economic moats. The remainder struggle to generate decent returns on capital, and those that do have only fleeting success.

Consider American Axle, which makes—you guessed it—axles for General Motors and Chrysler. Five years ago, when Americans couldn't buy SUVs fast enough, the company cranked out respectable returns on capital in the low to mid-teens. But since 2003, shrinking SUV sales and an uncompetitive cost structure have caused losses and crushed returns on capital to single-digit levels. The same story, with minor variations, could be repeated for many auto-parts manufacturers, which operate in a cutthroat industry with truly awful economics.

Turning to asset management, Morningstar covers 18 publicly traded asset managers, all of which have economic moats. (In fact, a dozen have wide moats, while the rest have narrow moats.)* Although the barriers to *entry* are low in asset management—anyone willing to spend $100,000 or so on lawyers and registration fees can start a mutual fund—the barriers to *success* are quite high, because it generally takes a large distribution network to really rake in the assets. However, those assets tend to stick around once they're in the door, which means that money managers that have amassed a good-sized pile of assets under management can generally generate high returns on capital without breaking much of a sweat.

Let's consider something akin to a worst-case scenario for an asset manager. Imagine a firm that specializes in one style of investing, and that style goes out of favor, making once-stellar returns turn into terrible ones. A few years later, it comes to light that the company has allowed big clients to trade its funds in a way that siphons profits from long-term fund holders, which embroils the company in a high-profile legal snafu. Star managers leave,

---

*At Morningstar, we divide companies with competitive advantages into two groups. Companies with very durable competitive advantages are labeled "wide moat," and companies with identifiable but less strong advantages are labeled "narrow moat." More on separating one from the other in Chapter 11, where we'll walk through several examples.

many investors follow suit, and assets under management are cut almost in half.

Doomsday? Hardly—this scenario is exactly what happened to Janus in the early part of the decade, and after dipping to 11 percent in the trough of the crisis, operating margins recovered to about 25 percent. That's what you call a resilient business model—one with a moat.

Looking for Moats in All the Right Places

Exhibit 9.1 breaks out Morningstar's coverage universe of more than 2,000 stocks into sectors, so we can see which areas of the market tend to have the most moats.

EXHIBIT 9.1   Moats by Sector

Sector	Narrow Moats (%)	Wide Moats (%)	All Moats (%)
Software	49	9	58
Hardware	26	5	31
Media	69	14	83
Telecommunications	59	0	59
Health Care Services	31	11	42
Consumer Services	32	7	39
Business Services	36	13	49
Financial Services	54	14	68
Consumer Goods	32	14	46
Industrial Materials	31	3	34
Energy	55	6	61
Utilities	80	1	81

In technology, you can see that software companies tend to have an easier time creating moats than hardware companies. This is not simply an accounting artifact—hardware firms are generally more capital-intensive than software firms—but has a strong basis on the way these two broad categories of products are used. A piece of software often needs to be integrated with other pieces of software to work properly, and this integration leads to customer lock-in and higher switching costs. Hardware is more frequently based on common industry standards, and can be swapped out for new hardware with less effort. There are important exceptions, of course, especially when a hardware company—like, say, Cisco Systems—is able to embed software in its products and create switching costs. But you'll generally find more moats among software companies than among hardware companies.

Given the turmoil in telecommunications over the past several years, it's a bit surprising to see that almost two-thirds of the telecom companies that we cover have moats, but there's a simple explanation: More than half of the telecom companies Morningstar covers are foreign, and they are often located in countries where the regulatory environment is more benign than here in the United States. In general, moats in the telecom sector are highly dependent on having either a favorable regulatory structure or a niche position that is not attractive to potential competitors, such as some of the carriers located in rural parts of the United States. But if you are looking for a telecom company with a competitive advantage, your best bet is to look abroad.

Although some media companies have been under siege recently, the industry is still a reasonably good hunting ground for companies with competitive advantages. Companies such as Disney and Time Warner, for example, control vast amounts of unique content that may cost a lot to produce initially, but which costs almost nothing to redistribute ad infinitum. In general, we've found that diversity and control of distribution channels help media companies create competitive advantage and a buffer against the inevitable loss of popularity of any individual media property. More so than many other sectors, however, many media companies are threatened with technological disruption as the Internet blows up well-established business models. Companies with extremely strong brands (Disney) or broad distribution networks (Comcast) seem like they will have the best chance of surviving with moats intact.

Like telecom companies, health care companies also face regulatory challenges—a change in Medicare's reimbursement rules can alter smaller companies' economics overnight—but the product diversity of larger firms mitigates this risk. Don't let the apparently small percentage of companies with moats in the table above fool you, because the large number of tiny biotech and single-product companies in the health care sector skews the data. Generally, you'll find more moats among companies that sell health care products, like drugs or medical devices, than you will among health maintenance organizations (HMOs) and hospitals that provide health care services. It's often harder to differentiate a service offering relative to a product that requires years or research and development plus Food and Drug Administration (FDA) approval to reach the market. And while the giant drug and device companies usually have solid competitive advantages, don't overlook smaller health care companies that often build very solid moats by dominating a niche— like Respironics and ResMed in sleep apnea, or Gen-Probe in blood testing.

Companies that cater directly to the consumer, like restaurants and retailers, often have a very hard time building competitive advantages—the percentage of consumer services companies with wide moats is one of the smallest of all the market sectors. The culprit here is low switching costs, because walking down the street from one shop or cafe to another is incredibly easy, and popular concepts can almost always be copied with ease. Popular fashion retailers or restaurant chains often present the illusion of a moat due to their fast growth and the buzz that surrounds a new type of store that is opening up several new locations every month, but be wary, because the odds are good that a knockoff concept is not far off. The moats that do exist in consumer services—companies like Bed Bath & Beyond, Best Buy, Target, or Starbucks— are generally the result of getting a lot of little things consistently right for years, which results in the kind of dependable consumer experience that drives loyalty and repeat traffic. It can be done, but it's not easy.

Companies that provide services to businesses are in many ways the polar opposite of the restaurants and retailers. This sector has one of the highest percentages of wide-moat companies in Morningstar's coverage universe, and that's largely because these firms are often able to integrate themselves so tightly into their clients' business processes that they create very high switching costs, giving them pricing power and excellent returns on capital. Data processors like DST Systems and Fiserv fall into this category, as do companies with impossible-to-replicate databases, like IMS Health (prescription drugs) or Dun & Bradstreet and Equifax (credit histories). This part of the market also has an outsize number of niche-dominating firms like Stericycle (medical waste), Moody's Investors Service (bond ratings), FactSet (financial data aggregation), and Blackbaud (fund-raising software for nonprofits). Although business services firms may be further from your everyday radar screen, they're usually worth the effort it takes to get to know them, given how rich in moats the sector tends to be.

The financial-services sector is another great place to look for companies with moats. Barriers to entry are quite high in some areas—who is going to start up a bulge-bracket investment bank to compete with Goldman Sachs, Lehman Brothers, and their ilk?—and switching costs protect the profits of even your most average bank, as we discussed in Chapter 4. Sticky assets lead to very durable returns on capital at almost every asset manager, and financial exchanges like the Chicago Merc and the NYMEX reap huge benefits from the network effect. Moats are harder to dig in the insurance industry, despite wide-moat outliers like Progressive Casualty Insurance Company and American International Group (AIG), because the products are more commodity-like and the switching costs are quite low. Also, many smaller specialty lenders and real estate investment trusts have a tough time building durable competitive advantages. Like business services companies, financial firms can take more work to understand—for one thing, their financial statements look very different than those of most companies—but the potential returns make the effort worthwhile. Moats abound in this area of the market.

Consumer goods is the home of many of the companies Warren Buffett has called "the inevitables"—companies such as Coca-Cola, Colgate-Palmolive, Wrigley, and Procter & Gamble, with incredibly durable brands and products that don't go out of style. Along with financial services, this sector has one of the highest percentages of wide-moat firms. It is easy to see why: Brands like Doublemint gum and Colgate toothpaste aren't built overnight, and it takes a lot of capital to maintain them through advertising and constant innovation. The sector is another great place to look for moats, but be wary of firms where the brand's value may be fleeting (clothing manufacturers like Kenneth Cole or Tommy Hilfiger), private-label products may threaten (Kraft or Del Monte), or low-cost labor may be permanently altering the industry's economics (Ethan Allen or Steelcase). And while "the inevitables" may be the best known, don't ignore niche-dominating companies like McCormick & Company (spices), Mohawk Industries (carpets), Tiffany (jewelry), or Sealed Air (packaging).

When cost is all that matters, it's tough for many companies in an industry to dig a moat, which is one of the big reasons that we see so few moats in industrial materials. Whether you are mining for metal, producing chemicals, making steel, or banging out auto parts, it is very hard to differentiate your product from those sold by your competitors, which means that all your customers care about is price. And like it or not, only a few companies in any commodity industry can truly have sustainable cost advantages.

In the metals area, we find that only the biggest of the big—companies like BHP Billiton and Rio Tinto—are able to create moats.

Don't write off industrial companies entirely, though—because that's what many investors do. Those willing to dig can find some real gems in this part of the market. What is especially attractive is that many investors in industrial stocks tend to treat them as a monolithic group that you buy when the economy is getting stronger and sell when it's getting weaker. Although it is true that many companies in this sector are sensitive to the overall economy, the tendency of the market to throw the baby (firms with moats) out with the bathwater (no-moat companies) can create big opportunities for those of us who look for competitive advantage. After all, this sector is home to niche-dominating firms like Graco (industrial pumps) and Nalco (water treatment), cost-advantaged companies like Steel Dynamics (steel) and Vulcan (construction aggregates), and companies that benefit from significant switching costs, like General Dynamics (defense) and Precision Castparts (advanced metal forgings). There are plenty of moats in the old economy, if you know what to look for.

On the surface, energy stocks seem much like commodity metals, but moats are more prevalent here than you might think for two reasons. First, companies that specialize in producing natural gas benefit from the difficulty of transporting gas over long distances. Although copper or even coal can be shipped around the world pretty easily, natural gas can really only be transported economically via pipeline—and pipelines don't cross oceans. As a result, natural-gas producers in North America can create moats by having lower costs than their nearby competitors, because they don't need to compete against supercheap natural gas coming out of the Middle East. So, North American gas producers can create moats by developing reserves that are low on the cost curve and have a reasonable life. Unlike natural gas, oil is traded globally—but also unlike natural gas, there's this cartel called the Organization of Petroleum Exporting Countries (OPEC) that does a pretty good job at keeping the price of oil relatively high. Those high prices create decent returns on capital for many (not all) oil producers, in addition to the fact that only a small number of well-capitalized giants have the resources to develop the increasingly hard-to-access oil fields that are being discovered.

We also find lots of moats in a small niche of the energy sector that is, surprisingly, not all that well-known: pipelines. Many of the companies that operate the vast network of pipelines used to transport natural gas, gasoline, crude oil, and a variety of other energy-related products trade publicly, and they are pretty good businesses. Generally, building a pipeline requires regulatory approval, which is not always easy to secure, and many pipelines benefit from the same niche economics discussed in Chapter 7: When there is not enough demand between two points to profitably support multiple pipelines, a single pipeline enjoys a local monopoly and can charge the maximum allowed rates. Moreover, those allowed rates can be fairly attractive, because pipelines have a somewhat looser regulatory regimen than utilities have. Pipelines are generally wrapped into a structure known as a master limited partnership, which can cause some tax complications for investors, and which is generally unsuitable for tax-deferred accounts like individual retirement accounts (IRAs) or 401(k)s. Still, the attractive returns and moaty businesses in this corner of the energy market make it worth an extra hour or two come tax time.

Finally, we come to utilities, which are a bit odd in terms of economic moats. Their natural monopolies over some geographic areas would seem to make them wide-moat businesses, but regulatory agencies have—unfortunately for investors, fortunately for consumers—figured this out, which is why their returns on capital are usually capped at a relatively low level. Reasonably friendly regulators are the best asset a utility can have, and this varies considerably by region—the Northeast and West Coast have some of the least friendly regulators, while the Southeast is a more benign environment. Generally speaking, the utility sector is not an area of the market where moats are abundant, but low-cost generating assets and friendly regulators can create decent returns, if you're careful about the price you pay.

Measuring a Company's Profitability

I hope you understand by now that moats increase the value of companies by helping them stay profitable for a longer period of time. So, what is the best way to measure a company's profitability? Easy—we look at how much profit the company is generating *relative to* the amount of money invested in the business. From a numbers perspective, this is the real key to separating great companies from average ones, because the job of any company is to take money and invest it in projects, products, or services to generate more money. The more capital that comes out relative to the amount that goes in, the better the business.

Understanding how much economic profit a company generates per *dollar of capital employed* tells us how efficiently a company is using its capital. More efficient capital users are going to be better businesses—and better investments— because they can increase shareholder wealth at a faster compound rate.

Think about it this way. A company's management is similar to the management of a mutual fund. A mutual fund manager takes investors' money and invests it in stocks or bonds to generate a return, and a manager who is able to generate, say, 12 percent returns is going to increase shareholders' wealth faster than a manager who can compound at only 8 percent. Companies aren't much different. They take shareholders' money and invest it in their own businesses to create wealth. By measuring the return that a company has achieved, we know how good it is at efficiently transforming capital into profits.

So, how do we measure return on capital? The three most common ways are return on assets (ROA), return on equity (ROE), and return on invested capital (ROIC). Each gives us the same information, but in a slightly different way.

Return on assets (ROA) measures how much income a company generates per dollar of assets, and if all companies were just big piles of assets, we could use it and be perfectly happy. It's a fine starting point, and you can find it calculated for just about any company on web sites such as Morningstar.com and elsewhere. Very broadly speaking, a nonfinancial company that can consistently generate an ROA of 7 percent or so likely has some kind of competitive advantage over its peers.

But many firms are at least partially financed with debt, which gives their returns on capital a leverage component that we need to take into account. Enter return on equity (ROE), which is also a great overall measure of returns on capital. ROE measures the efficiency with which a company uses shareholders' equity—think of it as measuring profits per dollar of shareholders' capital. One flaw of ROE is that companies can take on a lot of debt and boost their ROE without becoming more profitable, so it's a good idea to look at ROE alongside how much debt a company has. Like ROA, you can find ROE calculated for most companies on just about any financial web site. Again, as a very broad rule of thumb, you might use 15 percent as a reasonable cutoff—companies that can consistently crank out ROEs of 15 percent or better are more likely than not to have economic moats.

Finally, there's return on invested capital (ROIC), which combines the best of both worlds. It measures the return on all capital invested in the firm, regardless of whether it is equity or debt. So, it incorporates debt—unlike ROA—but removes the distortion that can make highly leveraged companies look very profitable using ROE. It also uses a different definition of profits that helps remove any effects caused by a company's financing decisions (debt versus equity), so we can get as close as possible to a number that represents the true efficiency of the underlying business. There are a number of ways to calculate

ROIC, and the formula can be complicated, so it is not a readily available number like ROA and ROE. The upshot is that you should interpret ROIC the same way as ROE and ROA—a higher return is preferable to a lower one.

Go Where the Money Is

Moats increase the value of companies because they enable companies to stay profitable for a longer stretch of time. And we want to measure profitability using return on capital, because companies that use capital efficiently will increase shareholders' capital at a faster clip. That sounds reasonable, but moats are more than just a tool for finding stronger, more valuable companies. As such, they should always be a core part of your stock-picking process.

But remember, you don't need to invest in every part of the stock market. Feeling the need to follow the herd and be exposed to this or that industry without regard to whether the industry's economics are attractive is a bad idea. Willie Sutton famously robbed banks because "that's where the money is." As an investor, you should strive to remember Willie's reasoning—some industries are structurally more profitable than others, and that's where the moats are. Your long-term investment dollars should follow.

The Bottom Line

1. It's easier to create a competitive advantage in some industries than it is in others. Life is not fair.
2. Moats are absolute, not relative. The fourth-best company in a structurally attractive industry may very well have a wider moat than the best company in a brutally competitive industry.

The Big Boss

*Management Matters Less
Than You Think.*

WHEN IT COMES to economic moats, management doesn't matter as much as you might think.

This may seem like a shocking statement to those used to seeing high-profile CEOs on the cover of business magazines and on television. But it's true. Long-term competitive advantages are rooted in the structural business characteristics that I laid out in Chapters 3 to 7, and managers have only a limited amount of ability to affect them. Sure, we can all remember the standouts in tough industries—heck, Starbucks managed to dig an economic moat around a chain of coffee shops—but these companies are much more the exceptions than the rule. (Remember the 1990s craze for bagel chains? No? Exactly.)

This point of view stands in direct opposition to the words of well-known business writer Jim Collins, who echoed many other business pundits when he wrote, "Greatness, it turns out, is largely a matter of conscious choice."

Well, no. "Conscious choice" can't turn a struggling auto-parts company into a highly profitable data processor any more than I can turn myself into Warren Buffett by drinking Cherry Coke and eating See's Candies. Nine times out of 10, the competitive dynamics of an industry will have a much greater impact on whether a company has an economic moat than any managerial decision. This is not because most managers are incompetent, but rather because some industries are less competitive than others; the cold, hard truth is that some CEOs just have an easier job maintaining high returns on capital.

As I discussed in Chapter 9, some industries are simply much more conducive to digging a moat than others. Throw a dart at a random asset manager, bank, or data processor, and I'll almost guarantee that you'll see higher long-run returns on capital than a randomly selected auto-parts company, retailer, or technology hardware company.

As much as business schools and management gurus would like us to believe that following some simple set of best practices will enable good companies to become great ones, it's just not true. Granted, smart management can enable a good company to become a better one, and I'd rather own a company with intelligent capital allocators at the helm than one run by a bunch of bozos. And dumb managers can certainly cause great companies to become less so. However, it's very rare for managerial decisions to have a bigger impact on a company's long-run competitive advantage than that company's structural characteristics.*

Think back to the Janus example in Chapter 9. Management did everything possible to run the business badly, yet profitability returned to high levels after a few years in the dumps. Or look at H&R Block, which earns fat returns on capital from a great tax-preparation franchise,

---

*You might think this would be different at a start-up company, because management could have a greater impact at a smaller and younger firm, but some recent research from University of Chicago Professor Steven Kaplan suggests that's not the case. In a recent paper ("Should Investors Bet on the Jockey or the Horse? Evidence from the Evolution of Firms from Early Business Plans to Public Companies," CRSP Working Paper 603, August 2007), he and his co-authors conclude that "at the margin, investors in start-ups should place more weight on investing in a strong business than on a strong management team."

despite pouring capital into sinkholes like Olde Discount Brokerage. Or McDonald's, which fell woefully out of touch with consumer tastes and for a time let customer service fall to unacceptable levels, yet was able to turn the business around relatively quickly based on the enduring strength of the McDonald's brand. In all three of these examples, a structural competitive advantage proved to be much more important in the long run than sub-par managerial decisions.

Now think about what happened when superstar CEOs like Jacques Nasser, Paul Pressler, or Gary Wendt tried to turn around Ford, the Gap, and Conseco, respectively. They met with complete failure in all three cases—bankruptcy, in Conseco's—and it wasn't for lack of trying or failure of managerial intelligence. There is just not much you can do with an automaker with structurally higher costs than the competition, a fashion retailer with an out-of-date brand, or a lender with too many bad loans on its books. The best engineer in the world can't build a 10-story sandcastle. The raw materials just aren't there.

As he often does, Warren Buffett summed this dynamic up best when he said, "When management with a reputation for brilliance tackles a business with a reputation for bad economics, it is the reputation of the business that remains intact."

Perhaps my very favorite example of a well-regarded CEO being humbled by brutal industry dynamics is David Neeleman at JetBlue. Neeleman had an impeccable track record when he founded JetBlue. Before that he had started up the only airline attractive enough to be purchased by the famously acquisition-shy Southwest Airlines, and then he helped launch a low-cost carrier in Canada while waiting for his noncompete agreement with Southwest to expire. When JetBlue launched, Neeleman's planes were brand-new and featured in-seat satellite TV and leather seats. Because new planes invariably have lower costs than older planes—they need less maintenance and they're more efficient—JetBlue's financials looked great just after going public, with 17 percent operating margins and a solid 20 percent return on equity.

Unfortunately, time doesn't stand still, and JetBlue's cost structure had nowhere to go but up, as its planes aged and employees accumulated tenure. Also, amenities like leather seats are relatively easy to copy—which, in fact, Southwest promptly did. Network airlines, emboldened by strong postbankruptcy balance sheets, engaged in price wars with JetBlue on some routes, and JetBlue's operating margins plunged. As of this writing, the shares are about 30 percent below their IPO price from five years ago, and despite a few less-than-stellar managerial decisions, the firm's performance is largely not Neeleman's fault. The airline industry simply has brutal economics, and that's what ultimately determined the company's difficulties.

The Celebrity CEO Complex

So why is that CEOs typically receive so much attention from investors? There are two reasons, one obvious and one insidious.

The obvious one is that the business media need to attract an audience, and CEOs are an easy subject. Who wouldn't want to read a story about the CEO of a Fortune 500 company that is posting record profits, or watch an interview with an executive about a company's successful international expansion strategy? The executives are typically happy to have the publicity, and the business reporter is happy to oblige by writing a topical story about a company of interest. It's a win-win for both parties, but it's often a disservice to investors who get the idea that these executives control the fate of their companies the way a star chef controls the output of his or her kitchen. Unfortunately, even Charlie Trotter would be challenged by the ingredients available in the kitchen of a local diner, and even a brilliant CEO has limited latitude for change in a brutal industry.

The insidious reason that managers get so much attention as the arbiters of corporate fate is that we are all biased. It's inherent in human nature to want to tell stories and see patterns that may not actually exist—we feel better when we can identify a cause for every effect that we observe, and identifying the causal agent as a single person is infinitely more satisfying than blaming a "lack of competitive advantage." The truth of the matter, though, is that CEOs have a hard time either creating a competitive advantage where it doesn't exist or damaging a competitive advantage that is very strong to begin with.

It is very easy as an investor to remember the exceptions—those companies that managed to dig moats in tough industries, often through the vision of a talented CEO. Companies like Starbucks, Dell, Nucor, Bed, Bath, and Beyond, and Best Buy all created substantial amounts of shareholder wealth by thriving in extremely brutal industries. But by anchoring on the success of companies like these and assuming their experiences are the rule rather than the exception, we confuse the *possible* with the *probable*. That's not good, because a big part of successful investing is stacking the odds in your favor.

The odds of a negative surprise from a company with a moat and mediocre management are far lower than from a company with no moat run by a CEO who may be the next Jack Welch. Assuming you've been careful in your competitive analysis, the firm with a moat stands a very strong chance of retaining its competitive advantage—management may surprise on the upside, or it may turn out to be worse than you had expected, but you have the moat as your backstop. The no-moat company, in contrast, has to overcome larger odds to succeed—management needs to be just as good as you expect (if not better) in order to succeed in a tough competitive environment, and if the CEO turns out to be a lesser light, the company's performance has nowhere to go but down.

Think about it this way: Which is easier to change, the industry a company is in or its managers? The answer, course, is obvious—executives come and go with regularity, but a company in a tough industry is stuck there for good. And since we know that some industries have structurally better economics than others, it stands to reason that the industry in which a company operates will likely have a bigger impact on its ability to generate high and sustainable returns on capital than will the CEO at the helm.

Management matters, but within boundaries set by companies' structural competitive advantages. No CEO operates in a vacuum, and while great managers can add to the value of a business, management by itself is not a sustainable competitive advantage.

The Bottom Line

1. Bet on the horse, not the jockey. Management matters, but far less than moats.
2. Investing is all about odds, and a wide-moat company managed by an average CEO will give you better odds of long-run success than a no-moat company managed by a superstar.

Chapter Eleven

Where the Rubber Meets the Road

~

Five Examples of
Competitive Analysis.

IN COLLEGE and in graduate school, I stunk at theory. Big-picture, abstract concepts went in one ear and out the other unless I could hang those ideas on concrete examples. I studied a lot of political science in graduate school, and although I slogged through the great political thinkers like Max Weber, Karl Marx, and Émile Durkheim,

I can't say I enjoyed them (aside from Joseph "creative destruction" Schumpeter, of course). By contrast, I loved reading books that took diverse bits of evidence and teased out a unifying theme or theory from the ground up. I've never really connected the dots before, but it was in hindsight a good prelude to a career as a bottom-up fundamental securities analyst.

In this chapter, I want to take all of the ideas about economic moats that I've thrown out so far and put them to the test by looking at five companies one by one, from the bottom up. After all, this is how you'll likely apply the ideas from this book in real life. You'll read about a company in a business magazine or hear it mentioned by a portfolio manager or colleague, and you'll be intrigued enough to do a little digging on your own. With that in mind, I picked the companies in this chapter in as realistic a manner as I could think of—I grabbed a few recent issues of major investing publications like *Fortune* and *Barron's,* and picked five companies that were mentioned favorably.

Exhibit 11.1 shows the three-step process I'll be using to determine whether these companies have moats. Step one is "show me the money"—has the company generated decent returns on capital in the past? When you're analyzing this, look at returns on capital over as long a period of time as possible, as a poor year or two does not disqualify

EXHIBIT 11.1 The Moats Process

Step 1	Step 2	Step 3
Has the firm historically generated solid returns on capital?	Does the firm have one or more of the competitive advantages listed below?	How strong is the company's competitive advantage? Is it likely to last a long time or a relatively short time?

Step 1 — No → Is the firm's future likely to be different than its past? — No → **No Economic Moat** — Yes →

Step 1 — Yes →

Step 2:
High Switching Costs   Network Economics
Low-Cost Production   Intangible Assets

Step 2 — No → **No Economic Moat**

Step 2 — Yes →

Step 3 — Short → **Narrow Moat**

Step 3 — Long → **Wide Moat**

a company from having a moat. (You can see 10 years of financial data free on Morningstar.com.)

If not, and the future is not likely to be appreciably different from the past, there is no moat. After all, a competitive advantage should show up in the numbers, and a firm that has not yet demonstrated the ability to earn an excess economic return is not one to pin your hopes on. It is possible that a company that has posted subpar returns on capital in the past may be poised for better days going forward, but such optimism would need to be accompanied by a large and positive shift in the underlying economics of the business. It does happen, and you can make a lot of money by identifying companies that have structurally changed for the better, but companies like these are much more the exception than the rule.

So no evidence of solid returns on capital generally equals no moat. But if a company has posted good returns on capital, our job becomes trickier. Step two in the process is identifying a competitive advantage—that is, figuring out why the company has been able to fend off competitors and generate excess economic returns. After all, it's entirely possible that even a company with a record of good returns on capital might not have a moat if there's no specific reason why those returns will persist into the future. If we didn't think about why high returns will stay high, we would just be driving by looking in the rearview mirror, which is rarely a good idea. Think about retailers and restaurant chains—switching costs for consumers are extremely low, so companies in these industries need scale, a well-established brand, or some other defensible advantage to give them a moat. Without an advantage, those high returns on capital could dissipate very quickly—history is full of hot retail or restaurant concepts that have flopped after a few years of early success.

This second step is where we need to apply all of the tools of competitive analysis. Does the company have a brand? Patents? Is it tough for customers to switch to competing products? Does it have sustainably lower costs? Does it benefit from network economics? Is it subject to technological disruption or a shift in industry dynamics? And so forth.

Assuming we've found some evidence of competitive advantage, step three is figuring out just how durable that advantage is likely to be. Some moats are real, but they may be easy to bridge, while some are wide enough that we can forecast high returns on capital for many years into the future with confidence. This is without question a subjective call, which is why I don't advocate slicing things too finely. At Morningstar, we divide companies into just three categories: wide moat, narrow moat, and no moat. I'll do the same in the examples that follow.

Now, let's put these ideas into action.

Hunting for Moats

Our first example is Deere & Company, which makes the eponymous agricultural equipment and also has a fair-sized segment selling construction machinery. As you can see in Exhibit 11.2, Deere has cranked out some pretty solid returns on capital over the past decade, despite a nasty downturn from 1999 to 2002. Agriculture is a cyclical business, so this shouldn't be too much of a concern—if Deere sold something with much steadier demand, like cheese or beer, we'd want to investigate further. So, based on the numbers, it looks like Deere has a moat.

Now we move on to competitive analysis—what is it about Deere that has allowed it to generate solid returns on capital, and are those returns likely to be sustained into the future? Well, the brand certainly helps. The company has been around for 170 years, and farmers are typically extremely loyal to the Deere brand. However, users of products from Deere's competitors, Case Construction Equipment and New Holland, are loyal, too, so there must be more to the story.

EXHIBIT 11.2   Deere & Company

Deere & Company DE	97	98	99	00	01	02	03	04	05	06	TTM	Avg
Net Margin (%)	7.5	7.4	2.0	3.7	−0.5	2.3	4.1	7.0	6.6	7.7	7.3	—
Return on Assets (%)	6.2	6.0	1.3	2.6	−0.3	1.4	2.6	5.1	4.6	5.0	4.5	3.5
Financial Leverage	3.9	4.4	4.3	4.8	5.7	7.5	6.6	4.5	4.9	4.6	4.7	—
Return on Equity (%)	24.9	24.8	5.9	11.6	−1.5	8.9	18.0	27.1	21.9	23.6	20.8	16.9

The key, as it turns out, is Deere's vast dealer network, which is much more extensive in North America than those of competitors. Dealers can quickly source parts and complete repairs on Deere equipment, which minimizes downtime during critical planting and harvesting seasons. The ability to get broken equipment up and running in short order is critical given that Deere's customers are extremely time-sensitive—a farmer might use a $300,000 combine for only a few weeks out of the year, but the machine absolutely, positively has to be running smoothly during those few weeks. Because replicating this dealer network would be possible for a competitor, and farmers might switch brands if Deere's quality slipped substantially, it's hard to say that Deere has a wide economic moat. But it would take years for a competitor to be able to do this, and it's not certain that a competitor actually will. So, I'd say Deere has a narrow but solid economic moat, and we can have some confidence that the company will continue to generate solid returns on capital for some time into the future.

Our next example takes us from the heartland to the Hamptons—Martha Stewart Living Omnimedia, which licenses the Martha Stewart brand and also produces magazines and TV shows. Given Martha's popularity—even after a brief sojourn in the pokey—we might expect the company to be pretty profitable. Let's check the numbers by referring to Exhibit 11.3.

EXHIBIT 11.3   Martha Stewart Living Omnimedia

Martha Stewart MSO	99	00	01	02	03	04	05	06	TTM	Avg
Net Margin (%)	11.0	7.5	7.4	2.5	−1.1	−31.8	−36.2	−5.9	−9.3	—
Return on Assets (%)	9.1	7.4	7.2	2.3	−0.9	−20.8	−29.2	−7.1	−12.6	−5.0
Financial Leverage	1.4	1.5	1.4	1.4	1.3	1.4	1.6	1.7	1.8	—
Return on Equity (%)	12.8	10.8	10.5	3.2	−1.2	−28.1	−43.5	−11.7	−22.6	−7.8

Hmm. Not very impressive, are they? At first glance, it's a bit of a concern that even in Martha's heyday, before she ran afoul of the law, the company generated less than a 13 percent return on equity. While that's not a terrible return on capital, we should expect better from a business that doesn't have a whole lot of invested capital to begin with. After all, Martha Stewart Living Omnimedia produces a magazine and a TV show, and licenses the brand to other companies; it doesn't own a whole bunch of factories or expensive inventory. So, despite the resurgent popularity of the Martha Stewart brand, I have to conclude that her company has no economic moat. And that's not a good thing.

Moving from a firm without much invested capital to one with a whole lot of it, let's take a look at Arch Coal, the country's second-largest coal producer. It's generally tough for commodity firms to dig an economic moat, so we'll probably be a bit skeptical when we start the analysis. Looking at the numbers, however, returns on capital have shown modest improvement to decent, if not great, levels. Looks like things started looking up for Arch in 2004, while both 2006 and 2007 showed solid results. See Exhibit 11.4.

Let's dig in further to see whether the past couple of years were an aberration, and returns on capital are likely to fall back to sub-par levels, or whether something has structurally changed for the better at Arch. First of all, it seems that Arch sold a bunch of money-losing mines in Central Appalachia in late 2005, which is positive for future returns on capital. Second, Arch is one of four companies that essentially control the supply of coal produced from an area called the Powder River Basin in Wyoming, and coal from this area is in demand from utilities because it has a very low sulfur content, and sulfur is one of the major pollutants that get emitted when coal is burned.

Now all of this is well and good, but if Arch were only competing with other firms producing coal in the Powder River Basin, it wouldn't have a moat unless it was producing coal at a sustainably lower cost than its peers in the area. (It's not, by the way.) However, coal from the

EXHIBIT 11.4   Arch Coal

Arch Coal ACI	97	98	99	00	01	02	03	04	05	06	TTM
Net Margin (%)	2.8	2.0	−22.1	−0.9	0.5	−0.2	1.2	6.0	1.5	10.4	7.3
Return on Assets (%)	1.8	1.3	−13.2	−0.6	0.3	−0.1	0.7	4.0	1.2	8.2	5.0
Financial Leverage	2.7	4.7	9.7	10.2	3.9	4.1	3.5	3.0	2.6	2.4	2.4
Return on Equity (%)	5.0	4.9	−80.6	−5.5	1.8	−0.5	2.7	12.9	3.4	20.5	12.0

Powder River Basin is much cheaper to produce than coal mined in many other parts of the U.S.—even after you take into account the higher transport costs, since the Powder River Basin is pretty far from high-population areas that consume lots of coal. And in a commodity business, if you can produce something at a sustainably lower cost than other companies selling the same product, you may very well have a moat.

So, why aren't we seeing this cost advantage in Arch's historical returns on capital? Well, it turns out that Arch signed some long-term contracts at much lower prices years ago, and those contracts are just starting to expire and be replaced by new contracts at much higher prices—which means that future returns on capital should be substantially higher than past returns. So, I think we can provisionally assign Arch a narrow economic moat, but it's a moat that we'd want to watch pretty closely. If production costs in the Powder River Basin increase considerably, or if the government introduces regulations that make coal less attractive as a resource by imposing a carbon tax, we'd want to re-evaluate things. But based on what we know today, Arch seems to have a (very) narrow moat.

Our fourth company isn't as well-known as the first three, but we can learn a lot about moats from looking at it. The Fastenal Company distributes a wide variety of maintenance, repair, and operations products to manufacturers and contractors around the United States. It does this through a network of about 2,000 stores, and specializes in fasteners, as the company's name implies. That may sound like a dull business, but let's check out the numbers to be sure. (See Exhibit 11.5.)

Wow! Whatever you might think of the business, those are not dull numbers. An average return on equity of more than 20 percent over a decade, with minimal financial leverage, is a highly uncommon achievement. In fact, out of the 3,000 stocks in Morningstar's database with market capitalizations over $500 million, only 50 have similar track records of generating tremendous returns on capital. The question, of course, is whether Fastenal just got lucky or built a competitive advantage that will allow it to maintain such high returns on capital.

When you dig into the company, it turns out that Fastenal benefits from location-based scale economies similar to the cement and aggregate companies discussed in Chapter 7. Fasteners, such as screws, anchors, and bolts,

EXHIBIT 11.5   Fastenal Company

Fastenal FAST	97	98	99	00	01	02	03	04	05	06	TTM	Avg
Net Margin (%)	10.3	10.5	10.8	10.8	8.6	8.3	8.5	10.6	11.0	11.0	11.1	—
Return on Assets (%)	22.9	23.2	23.0	22.4	16.0	14.6	13.9	18.4	20.1	20.6	19.0	19.5
Financial Leverage	1.2	1.2	1.1	1.1	1.1	1.1	1.1	1.1	1.1	1.1	1.2	—
Return on Equity (%)	28.0	27.6	26.2	25.2	17.9	16.3	15.6	20.8	22.7	23.3	21.7	22.3

are heavy and expensive to ship and they don't cost very much, which means that Fastenal gets a big cost advantage from having lots of stores close to its customers. Proximity also means that Fastenal usually has a quicker delivery time than competitors, which is another big advantage given that manufacturers typically need fasteners when something breaks, and downtime is a very expensive proposition for these firms.

With twice as many locations as its nearest competitor, Fastenal seems able to maintain its scale advantage, especially because it essentially dominates hundreds of small geographic niches that would not be profitable enough by themselves for a competitor to attack. The company also maintains an in-house truck fleet that allows it to distribute products to its stores—and to customers' job sites—at much lower cost than if it used a third-party shipper like UPS. So, to take on Fastenal, a competitor would need a similarly scaled distribution network plus a willingness to build noneconomic stores in Fastenal markets that are only large enough for a single distributor. That sounds like a pretty daunting task, which is why I think Fastenal is a wide-moat business with the potential to crank out a superior return on capital for many years into the future.

For the final example, I want to show you why it is so important to think about the competitive dynamics of a business, in addition to looking at its track record of generating solid returns on capital. If you had looked at either of these two businesses in 2004 or so, you would have licked your lips over the returns on capital. Company B's track record was not quite as consistent as Company A's, but the trend was certainly in the right direction. (See Exhibit 11.6 and Exhibit 11.7.)

Company A is Pier 1 Imports, and Company B is Hot Topic, two retailers that were hitting on all cylinders in the late 1990s and the early part of the current decade. Both were growing nicely—Hot Topic at a phenomenal 40+ percent pace, and Pier 1 at a more measured mid-teens rate—and both were cranking out very respectable

EXHIBIT 11.6   Company A

Company A	98	99	00	01	02	03	04	Avg
Net Margin (%)	7.3	7.1	6.1	6.7	6.5	7.4	6.3	—
Return on Assets (%)	12.8	12.3	11.3	12.9	12.5	14.1	11.7	12.5
Financial Leverage	1.7	1.6	1.5	1.4	1.5	1.5	1.5	—
Return on Equity (%)	21.8	20.2	17.7	17.8	17.9	21.1	21.1	19.2

EXHIBIT 11.7   Company B

Company B	98	99	00	01	02	03	04	Avg
Net Margin (%)	6.4	5.8	8.0	9.0	8.5	7.8	8.4	—
Return on Assets (%)	9.5	10.8	18.3	22.4	20.3	18.9	19.8	17.1
Financial Leverage	1.2	1.2	1.3	1.2	1.2	1.3	1.3	—
Return on Equity (%)	10.8	12.8	23.3	27.9	24.4	23.4	25.0	21.1

returns on capital. But let's think about the nature of their businesses. Pier 1 sells imported furniture and home accessories, and Hot Topic is a teen clothing retailer with a very specific look to its wares—both decent businesses, as long as the companies do a good job managing inventories and staying on top of consumer trends. However, it would have been a stretch to confidently predict that Pier 1 and Hot Topic could maintain such high returns on capital for a long time, as switching costs for their consumers are essentially nil.

It turns out that you would have been right to be skeptical. (See Exhibit 11.8 and Exhibit 11.9.)

EXHIBIT 11.8 Pier 1 Imports, Inc.

Pier 1 Imports, Inc. PIR (Company A)	05	06	07	TTM
Net Margin (%)	3.2	−2.2	−14.0	−16.3
Return on Assets (%)	5.6	−3.6	−21.8	−26.3
Financial Leverage	1.6	2.0	2.5	2.8
Return on Equity (%)	9.1	−6.4	−47.9	−60.5

EXHIBIT 11.9 Hot Topic, Inc.

Hot Topic, Inc. HOTT (Company B)	05	06	07	TTM
Net Margin (%)	6.0	3.1	1.8	1.8
Return on Assets (%)	14.2	7.8	4.4	4.0
Financial Leverage	1.5	1.5	1.4	1.5
Return on Equity (%)	19.3	11.5	6.5	6.1

Both companies have fallen off a cliff over the past few years, in terms of both returns on capital and stock price. (From early 2005 to mid-2007, Hot Topic's stock price was cut in half, and Pier 1's stock is down a painful 75 percent.) The story was the same in both cases—consumers stopped buying what the companies were selling as trends moved in different directions (and for Pier 1, competition heated up as well). Retail is a tough business—easy come, easy go.

Although I used retailers in this example, I could have picked a smaller technology company just as easily—or really any company without a structural competitive advantage. The point is that unless a company has some kind of economic moat, predicting how much shareholder value it will create in the future is pretty much a crapshoot, *regardless* of what the historical track record looks like. Looking at the numbers is a start, but it's only a start. Thinking carefully about the strength of the company's competitive advantage, and how it will (or won't) be able to keep the competition at bay, is a critical next step.

At this point, you have all the tools you need to start separating wonderful businesses from companies with more uncertain futures. But how will you know when those businesses are trading at attractive prices? That's the subject of our next two chapters.

The Bottom Line

1. To see if a company has an economic moat, first check its historical track record of generating returns on capital. Strong returns indicate that the company may have a moat, while poor returns point to a lack of competitive advantage—unless the company's business has changed substantially.

2. If historical returns on capital are strong, ask yourself how the company will maintain them. Apply the tools of competitive analysis from Chapters 3 to 7, and try to identify a moat. If you can't identify a specific reason why returns on capital will stay strong, the company likely does not have a moat.

3. If you can identify a moat, think about how strong it is and how long it will last. Some moats last for decades, while others are less durable.

Chapter Twelve

What's a Moat Worth?

*Even the Best Company Will
Hurt Your Portfolio If You Pay
Too Much for It.*

IF INVESTING WERE as simple as identifying wonderful businesses with economic moats, making money in the stock market would be a lot easier—and this book would be finished. But the reality is that the price you pay for a stock is critically important to your future investment returns, which is why step 2 of the game plan I wrote about way back on the first page of the Introduction read: "Wait until the shares of those businesses trade for less than their intrinsic value, and buy."

Valuation is a funny thing. I've met lots of very intelligent investors who could quote me chapter and verse about the companies whose shares they owned, or were thinking of buying, but couldn't answer a simple question: "So, what's it worth?" The same individuals who will haggle for hours over a car, or drive a mile out of their way to save a few cents per gallon on a tank of gas, will buy stocks with only a vague sense of the potential value of the business.

The reason for this, I think, is simply that valuing a stock is hard—and pretty uncertain, even for professionals—so most people just throw in the towel and don't try. After all, it's easy to know if a gas station or car dealer is giving you a good deal, because you know what similar products are selling for. If a dealer wants $40,000 for that new Lexus and other dealers are selling it for $42,000, it's the same car so you can be reasonably confident that you're not overpaying at $40,000. But in valuing companies, we run into two hurdles.

First, every company is slightly different, which makes comparisons tough. Growth rates, returns on capital, strength of competitive advantage, and a host of other factors all affect the value of a business, so comparing two companies with each other is likely to be a difficult exercise.

(It is useful in some cases—more on that later in this chapter.) Second, the value of a company is directly tied to its future financial performance, which is unknown, though we can obviously make some educated guesses. For these reasons, most people focus on the information that is easily attainable about stocks (their market prices) rather than the information that is harder to obtain (their business values).

That's the bad news. The good news is that you don't need to know the precise value of a company before buying its shares. All you need to know is that the current price is *lower* than the *most likely value* of the business. That may sound confusing, so let me give you an example.

In the summer of 2007, I noticed that a company I'd had on my radar screen for some years, called Corporate Executive Board, had dropped in price by about half over the previous year. The company had been growing sales and earnings at a blistering pace of over 30 percent per year for a few years, and for a variety of reasons, things hit a wall—sales growth slowed considerably, and earnings growth dropped to about 10 percent. I did some research, and I was convinced that the company had plenty of room left to grow in its market. I was also confident that Corporate Executive Board's competitive position was still very strong. Would the company return to its 30 percent growth rate, or would future growth be lower, say 15 percent?

I really didn't know, and the valuation of the shares was very different under those two scenarios.

So why did I buy the stock? Because while I did not know exactly what Corporate Executive Board's shares were worth, I did know that the stock price at the time implied that the market was assuming a 10 percent growth rate. So, my task was simply to decide how likely it was that the company would never grow faster than 10 percent. Based on my research, I thought that was a very unlikely outcome, and so I bought the stock. If the company returned to a 15 percent growth rate, my investment would do pretty well, and if the company returned to a 20+ percent growth rate, I'd have a home run. Only if the company decelerated to a single-digit growth rate would I lose money, and I thought the odds of that happening were acceptably low.

In this example, I reverse-engineered the price of the shares to see what kinds of growth expectations were baked in. The key takeaway is that I didn't have to know exactly what the future would bring; I just had to know that the future was very likely going to brighter than the share price implied. In the case of Corporate Executive Board, I thought the stock could be worth anywhere from $85 to $130, but I was confident that the stock would not be worth much less than its $65 share price. (Time will tell if I was right.)

The simple exercise of estimating the value of a share of a company is the key to buying stocks for less than their potential value, because in order to buy the shares for less than their value, you need to have some idea of what that value is. (It sounds simple, but you'd be amazed at how many investors have never tried to value the stocks they buy.)

What Is a Company Worth, Anyway?

It's a simple question, so here's a simple answer: A stock is worth the present value of all the cash it will generate in the future. That's it.

Let's pick this idea apart a bit. Companies create value by investing capital and generating a return on that investment. Some of the cash that a company generates pays operating expenses, some gets reinvested back in the business, and the remainder is what's called "free cash flow." Free cash flow is often called "owner earnings," because that's really what it is—the amount of money that could be extracted from a business every year by the firm's owners without harming the company's operations.

Think of free cash flow like the money a landlord clears at the end of every year. The owner of an apartment building gets rent (sales), pays for the mortgage and some annual upkeep (operating expenses), and occasionally spends some money for major repairs like a new roof or new windows (capital expenditures). What's left over is his or her personal free cash flow, which can be tucked away in a bank account, spent on a nice Florida vacation, or used to buy another apartment building. But whatever the landlord uses it for, it's not money that is needed to keep the apartment building functioning as a cash-generating enterprise.

Sticking with the landlord example, let's think about what would make a building full of rental apartments worth more or less to a prospective purchaser. Growth would certainly push the value up—if a building had an adjacent patch of land on which a landlord could build more apartments, it would be worth more than a building without that land, as the stream of potential future rental income would be larger. The same goes for the riskiness of the rental income—a building full of seasoned wage-earners would be worth more than the same building full of college students, because the landlord would be more confident of actually collecting the rent each month without a big hassle.

You'd also imagine that a higher return on capital would make a building worth more—if you thought you could raise rents in a certain building and essentially get more income with no investment, that property would be worth more than a building with stagnant rents. Finally, let's not forget competitive advantage—a building that was the last to go up before a zoning ordinance prevented adjacent new apartment buildings would be worth more than a building that potentially faced lots of new apartments competing with it.

Guess what? You've just learned the most important concepts that underpin the valuation of any company: the likelihood that those estimated future cash flows will actually materialize (risk), how large those cash flows will likely be (growth), how much investment will be needed to keep the business ticking along (return on capital), and how long the business can generate excess profits (economic moat). Keep these four factors in mind when using price multiples or any other valuation tool, and you're certain to make better investing decisions.

Invest, Don't Speculate

There are three types of tools for valuing companies: price multiples, yields, and intrinsic values. All three are valuable parts of the investing toolkit, and the wise investor will apply more than one to a prospective purchase. I'll go over price multiples and yields in the next chapter. (Intrinsic values are a bit more complicated, and generally require a somewhat technical method called discounted cash flow, which is a bit beyond the scope of this book.*)

---

*If you're interested in learning about how to calculate an intrinsic value, I'd recommend picking up another book I've written about investing, called *The Five Rules for Successful Stock Investing* (John Wiley & Sons, 2004), which goes into more detail on accounting and valuation.

However, understanding price multiples and yields will be easier if we first detour briefly into what drives stock returns. Over long stretches of time, there are just two things that push a stock up or down: The *investment return,* driven by earnings growth and dividends, and the *speculative return,* driven by changes in the price-earnings (P/E) ratio.

Think of the investment return as reflecting a company's financial performance, and the speculative return as reflecting the exuberance or pessimism of other investors. A stock might go from $10 to $15 per share because earnings have increased from $1 per share to $1.50 per share, or because even though earnings stayed flat at $1 per share, the P/E ratio increased from 10 to 15. In the first case, the stock was driven completely by investment return; in the latter case, the shares climbed solely due to speculative return.

When you focus your investment search on companies with economic moats, you're maximizing your potential investment return, because you're looking for companies that are likely to create economic value and increase their earnings over long periods of time.

By paying close attention to valuation, you're minimizing the risk of a negative speculative return—that is, the odds that a change in the mood of other investors will hurt your investment performance. After all, no one knows what a stock's speculative returns will be over the next five or 10 years, but we can make some pretty reasonable educated guesses about the investment return. Careful valuation will help insulate you against an adverse change in market emotion.

Let's look at a real-world example. As of mid-2007, Microsoft had increased earnings per share at an average rate of roughly 16 percent per year over the past decade. So, 16 percent was the company's 10-year average investment return. But Microsoft's shares have appreciated at an average annual rate of only about 7 percent over the same time period, which means its speculative return must have been negative, to drag down that juicy 16 percent investment return. In fact, that's precisely what happened—10 years ago, Microsoft shares were valued at a P/E ratio of 50, and today the P/E ratio is just 20.

Contrast Microsoft with Adobe, which produces Photoshop, Acrobat, and a host of other image-processing software products. Over the past decade, Adobe's earnings per share have increased at about 13 percent per year on average—that's the investment return. But the shares have appreciated at almost twice that rate, about 24 percent per year, because over the past 10 years the stock's P/E ratio changed from about 17 to about 45 today, which added a huge amount of speculative return.

As you can see, a change in the market's mood—the speculative return—caused a drastically different outcome for an investor who bought shares of two companies in the same industry that posted roughly the same growth rate over the past decade. The Microsoft investor has received returns roughly in line with the market, while the Adobe investor has made several times his or her initial investment.

Now, the Adobe example is an extreme; buying a stock with the expectation that the market will deliver a massive speculative return is folly. But by purchasing shares at a P/E of 17 a decade ago (versus a P/E of 50 for Mister Softee), the buyer of Adobe minimized the risk of the negative speculative return that whacked the buyer of Microsoft shares over the past 10 years. The fact that the lucky Adobe buyer benefited from a huge increase in the P/E ratio is gravy.

This is why valuation is so important. By paying close attention to valuation, you're maximizing the impact of something you can forecast (a company's financial performance) on your future investment returns, and minimizing the impact of something you can't forecast (the enthusiasm or pessimism of other investors). Besides, who doesn't like getting a deal?

The Bottom Line

1. A company's value is equal to all the cash it will generate in the future. That's it.

2. The four most important factors that affect the valuation of any company are how much cash it will generate (growth), the certainty attached to those estimated cash flows (risk), the amount of investment needed to run the business (return on capital), and the amount of time the company can keep competitors at bay (economic moat).

3. Buying stocks with low valuations helps insulate you from the market's whims, because it ties your future investment returns more tightly to the financial performance of the company.

Chapter Thirteen

Tools for Valuation

How to Find Stocks on Sale.

HAVING—I HOPE—CONVINCED YOU that valuation is critical to ensuring that your careful competitive analysis pays off in attractive portfolio returns, let's look at price multiples, our first tool. Multiples are simultaneously the most commonly used and the most commonly *misused* valuation tool.

The most basic multiple is the price-to-sales (P/S) ratio, which is just the current price of a stock divided by sales per share. The nice thing about the price-to-sales ratio is that just about all companies have sales, even when business is temporarily in the dumps—which makes P/S particularly useful for cyclical companies or companies that are having some kind of trouble that sends earnings temporarily into the red. The trick with the P/S ratio, however, is that a dollar of sales may be worth a little or a lot, depending on how profitable the company is. Low-margin businesses, such as retailers, typically have very low P/S ratios relative to high-margin businesses like software or pharmaceuticals. So, don't use price-to-sales ratios to compare companies in different industries, or you'll wind up thinking that the lowest-margin companies are all great bargains, while the high-margin ones are too expensive.

In my opinion, the P/S ratio is most useful for companies that have temporarily depressed margins, or that have room for a lot of improvement in margins. Remember that high margins mean more earnings per dollar of sales, which leads to a higher P/S ratio. So, if you run across a low-margin company with a P/S ratio in line with similar low-margin companies and you think the company can cut costs and boost profitability significantly, you might have a cheap stock in your sights.

In fact, one useful way to use the price-to-sales ratio is to find high-margin companies that have hit a speed bump. Companies that have been able to post fat margins in the past, but which have low current P/S ratios, may be discounted by the market because other investors assume the decline in profitability is permanent. If in fact the company can return to its former level of profitability, then the stock is probably quite cheap. This is one use for which the price-to-sales ratio can be a better tool than the price-earnings ratio; the P/E on a stock that is under-earning its potential would be high (because E is low), so looking for low P/Es wouldn't uncover these kinds of out-of-favor stocks.

Hitting the Books

The second common multiple is the price-to-book (P/B) ratio, which compares the company's market price with its book value, which is also called shareholders' equity. Think of book value as representing all the physical capital invested in the company—factories, computers, real estate, inventory, you name it. The rationale for using book value in certain cases is that future earnings and cash flows are ephemeral, while the stuff that a company physically owns has a more tangible and certain value.

The key to using the P/B ratio in valuing stocks is to think carefully about what "B" represents. Whereas a dollar of earnings or cash flow is exactly the same from Company A to Company B, the stuff that makes up book value can vary dramatically. For an asset-intensive firm like a railroad or a manufacturing firm, book value represents the bulk of the assets that generate revenue—things like locomotives, factories, and inventory. But for a service or technology firm, for example, the revenue-generating assets are people, ideas, and processes, none of which are generally contained in book value.

Moreover, many of the competitive advantages that create economic moats are typically not accounted for in book value. Take Harley-Davidson as an example, which has a P/B ratio of about 5 as of this writing, meaning that the company's current market value is about five times the rough net worth of its factories, land, and inventory of yet-to-be-built motorcycle parts. That seems pretty rich, until you consider that the value of the company's brand name is not accounted for in book value, and it's the brand that allows Harley to earn 25 percent operating margins and a 40 percent return on equity.

There is one other quirk to book value worth knowing. It can often be inflated by an accounting convention known as goodwill, which is created when one company buys another. Goodwill is the difference between the acquired company's tangible book value and the price paid for it by the buyer, and as you can imagine, it can be a huge number for firms without a lot of physical assets. (When America Online bought Time Warner, the book value of the combined firm increased by $130 *billion* in goodwill.) The trouble is, goodwill often represents little more than the desire of the acquiring firm to buy the target before someone else does, and so its value is usually debatable, to say the very least. You're best off subtracting goodwill from book value—and often when you see a price-to-book ratio that seems too good to be true, it's because a big goodwill asset is boosting book value.

So, with all these pitfalls, why bother with book value? Because it is extremely useful for one sector of the market that contains a disproportionate number of companies with solid competitive advantages: financial services. The assets of a financial company are typically very liquid (think of the loans on a bank's balance sheet), so they are very easy to value accurately, which means that the book value of a financial services company is usually a pretty decent approximation of its actual tangible value. The only caveat here is that an abnormally low price-to-book ratio for a financial firm can indicate that the book value is somehow in question—perhaps because the company made some bad loans that will need to be written off.

The Multiple That Is Everywhere

As you have no doubt guessed by now, every price multiple has a good side and a bad side—and the mother of all multiples, the price-earnings (P/E) ratio, is no different. Price-earnings ratios are useful because earnings are a decent proxy for value-creating cash flow, and because earnings results and estimates are readily available from just about any source you care to name. They are tricky, though, because earnings can be a noisy number, and because a price-earnings ratio doesn't mean a whole lot in a vacuum—a P/E of 14 is neither good nor bad, unless we know something about the company or we have a benchmark against which to compare the P/E.

Of course, one of the trickiest aspects of the price-earnings ratio is that, while there may be only one "P," there may be more than one "E." I've seen P/Es calculated using earnings from the most recent fiscal year, the current fiscal year, the current calendar year, the past four quarters, and estimates for the next fiscal year. Which one should you use?

That's a tough question. Always approach a forecasted earnings number with some caution. These forecasts are usually the consensus estimate of all Wall Street analysts following the company, and multiple studies have shown that consensus estimates are typically too pessimistic just before a beaten-down company rebounds, and too optimistic just before a highflier slows down. A reasonable-looking P/E of 15 becomes a less reasonable 20 if earnings turn out to be 25 percent less than expected.

My advice is to look at how the company has performed in good times and bad, do some thinking about whether the future will be a lot better or worse than the past, and come up with your own estimate of how much the company could earn in an average year. That's the best basis for a P/E on which to base your valuation because (1) it is your own, so you know what went into the forecast, and (2) it is based on an average year for the company, not the best of times or the worst of times.

Once you have found your "E," you are ready to use the P/E ratio. The most common way to use a P/E is to compare it with something else, such as a competitor, an industry average, the entire market, or the same company at another point in time. There is some merit to this approach, as long as you don't go about it blindly and you remember the four main drivers of valuation that I discussed earlier in the chapter: risk, growth, return on capital, and competitive advantage.

A company that is trading at a lower P/E than others in the same industry might be a good value—or it might deserve that lower P/E because it has lower returns on capital, less robust growth prospects, or a weaker competitive advantage. The same limitations apply to any comparison of a single company's price-earnings ratio with the average P/E of the whole stock market.

A company with a P/E of 20 relative to the market P/E of about 18 (as of mid-2007) looks a little pricey; but what if that company is, say, Avon Products, with a wide economic moat, 40 percent returns on capital, and robust growth prospects in emerging markets? Hmm—maybe the shares are not so pricey after all.

Similar cautions apply when comparing a company's current P/E with past price-earnings ratios. It is common for investors to justify an undervalued stock by declaring, "The shares are trading at their lowest multiple in a decade!" (I've done this more than a few times myself.) All else being equal, a company trading for 20 times earnings that has historically traded for 30 to 40 times earnings sounds like one heck of a deal—as long as it has the same growth prospects, returns on capital, and competitive position. But if any of those attributes has changed, then all bets are off. Past performance may not guarantee future results, after all.

Less Popular, but More Useful

Finally, there's my favorite price multiple, which uses cash flow from operations in the denominator, rather than earnings. Without getting into the gory accounting details, cash flow can present a more accurate picture of a company's profit potential because it simply shows how much cash is flowing in and out of a business, whereas earnings are subject to a lot of adjustments. For example, publishers usually have higher cash flow than earnings, because people pay for a year's worth of magazines before they actually receive them. By contrast, a business that that sells stuff on credit—say, a store selling plasma TVs—will have higher earnings than cash flow, because the store will record earnings as soon as you walk out the door with the TV, even though it won't get your cash until you send in your monthly installment payments.

As you might guess, it's pretty nice when your customers pay you *before* you have to do anything for them. Businesses with this characteristic—often subscription-based—tend to have higher cash flow than earnings, so while they may look expensive using a P/E ratio, they can look much more reasonably priced using a ratio of price to cash flow. (More often than not, these kinds of businesses also have high returns on capital.) For example, the company I used as an example in the previous chapter, Corporate Executive Board, typically reports about 50 percent more cash flow than earnings each year.

The ratio of price to cash flow is also useful because cash flow tends to be a bit steadier than earnings; for example, it is not affected by noncash charges that come from a corporate restructuring or an asset write-down. Also, cash flow takes capital efficiency into account in some ways, because companies that need less working capital to grow will usually have higher cash flow than earnings. One thing cash flow does not do is take depreciation into account, so asset-intensive companies will often have higher cash flow than earnings, which can overstate their profitability because those depreciated assets will need to be replaced someday.

That's it for the four most common multiples, the first type of tool in our valuation kit. A second useful group of tools is yield-based valuation metrics, which are great because we can compare them directly to an objective benchmark—bond yields.

Say Yes to Yield

If we turn the P/E on its head and divide earnings per share by a stock's price, we get an earnings yield. For example, a stock with a P/E of 20 (20/1), would have an earnings yield of 5 percent (1/20), and a stock with a P/E of 15 (15/1) would have an earnings yield of 6.7 percent (1/15). With 10-year Treasury bonds trading for about 4.5 percent in mid-2007, those both look like reasonably attractive rates of return relative to bonds. Of course, you're not guaranteed to receive the investment returns on those two stocks, whereas the T-bond is backed by Uncle Sam, a fairly trustworthy guy. However, you're balancing out the additional risk with something positive: The earnings stream from a company will generally grow over time, whereas the bond payments are fixed in stone. Life is full of trade-offs.

We can improve on an earnings yield with a neat little measure called the cash return, which is simply the annual cash yield you'd get if you bought a company, paid off all its debt, and kept the free cash flow. Going back to our apartment-building analogy from the preceding chapter, think of cash return as the income stream, as a percentage of the purchase price, that you might get from owning an apartment building outright after paying for maintenance and upkeep. Cash return tells us how much free cash flow a company is generating relative to the cost of buying the whole company, including its debt burden.

This measure improves on the earnings yield because it looks at free cash flow (owner earnings) and incorporates debt into the company's capital structure. To calculate cash return, add free cash flow (cash flow from operations, minus capital expenditures) to net interest expense (interest expense minus interest income). That's the top half of the ratio. The bottom half is called "enterprise value," which is the company's market capitalization (equity) plus long-term debt, minus any cash on the balance sheet. Divide free cash flow plus net interest by enterprise value, and there you go—cash return.

As an example, let's take a quick look at Covidien Ltd., a huge health-care company that was part of Tyco International before that company broke itself up. In 2007, Covidien posted about $2 billion in free cash flow, and it paid about $300 million in interest. So, $2 billion plus $300 million equals $2.3 billion, and there's the top half of the ratio. The company has a market cap of $20 billion and long-term debt of about $4.6 billion, and the sum of those numbers, less $700 million in cash on the balance sheet, is Covidien's enterprise value of $23.9 billion.

We divide $2.3 billion by $23.9 billion, and we get a cash return of 9.6 percent, which is pretty juicy considering that that cash stream should grow over time, because Covidien sells into a number of health-care markets with solid prospects.

So, now you have a number of valuation tools at your disposal—multiples and yields—and you should have an idea of when each is useful and when it's not. How do you put these together to decide whether the price of a stock is less than its value?

The short answer is "very carefully." The long answer is that it takes practice and a fair amount of trial and error to become skilled at identifying undervalued stocks, but I think the following five tips will give you better odds of success than most investors.

1. *Always remember the four drivers of valuation:* risk, return on capital, competitive advantage, and growth. All else being equal, you should pay less for riskier stocks, more for companies with high returns on capital, more for companies with strong competitive advantages, and more for companies with higher growth prospects.

   Bear in mind that these drivers compound each other. A company that has the potential to grow for a long time, with low capital investment, little competition, and reasonable risk, is potentially worth a *lot* more than one with similar growth prospects but lower returns on capital and an uncertain competitive outlook. Investors who focus blindly on the popular P/E-to-growth (PEG) ratio usually miss this key point, because they are forgetting that growth at a high return on capital is much more valuable than growth at a low return on capital.

2. *Use multiple tools.* If one ratio or metric indicates that the company is cheap, apply another as well. The stars won't always align, but when they do, it's a good indication that you've found a truly under-valued company.

3. *Be patient.* Wonderful businesses do not trade at great prices very often, but as Warren Buffett has said, "There are no called strikes in investing." Have a watch list of wonderful businesses that you would love to own at the right price, wait for that price, and then pounce. Although you don't want to be too picky—opportunity does have a cost—remember one thing when the decision is not clear: *Not making* money beats *losing* money any day of the week.

4. *Be tough.* The odds are good that the world will be telling you not to invest at precisely the time that you should. Wonderful businesses do not trade for

great prices when the headlines are positive and Wall Street is cheery; they get cheap when the news is bad and investors overreact. You'll have to buy when everyone else is selling, which is not easy. It is profitable, though, and that's the nice thing about it.

5. *Be yourself.* You will make better investment decisions based on your own hard-won knowledge about a company than you will decisions based on any pundit's tips. The reason is simple. If you understand the source of a company's economic moat and you think the business is trading for less than its value, it will be much easier for you to make the tough against-the-grain decisions required of a successful investor. If, however, you are constantly relying on the tips and advice of others without doing some research on your own, you'll be constantly questioning whether that advice is any good, and you'll probably buy high and sell low.

The best business in the world will be a bad investment if purchased at an unattractive price. Ask anyone who bought Coke or Cisco in 1999 or 2000—they were great businesses then, and they still are today, but their valuations were so high that there was no room for error or for profit. Buying a stock without close attention to valuation is like buying a car without looking at the sticker price. If you buy the car, at least you get to enjoy driving it, but buying stocks that are too expensive carries no such side benefit. Make sure valuation is a tailwind for your stock picks rather than a headwind.

The Bottom Line

1. The price-to-sales ratio is most useful for companies that are temporarily unprofitable or are posting lower profit margins than they could. If a company with the potential for better margins has a very low price-to-sales ratio, you might have a cheap stock in your sights.

2. The price-to-book ratio is most useful for financial services firms, because the book value of these companies more closely reflects the actual tangible value of their business. Be wary of extremely low price-to-book ratios, because they can indicate that the book value may be questionable.

3. Always be aware of which "E" is being used for a P/E ratio, because forecasts don't always come true. The best "E" to use is your own: Look at how the company has performed in good times and bad, think about whether the future will be

(continued)

a lot better or worse than the past, and come up with your own estimate of how much the company could earn in an average year.

4. Ratios of price to cash flow can help you spot companies that spit out lots of cash relative to earnings. It is best for companies that get cash up front, but it can overstate profitability for companies with lots of hard assets that depreciate and will need to be replaced someday.

5. Yield-based valuations are useful because you can compare the results directly with alternative investments, like bonds.

Chapter Fourteen

When to Sell

—— ❧ ——

Smart Selling Means
Better Returns.

Way back in the mid-1990s, I came across a small company called EMC Corporation that sold computer storage equipment. I did some research on the stock, and I decided that although it was a bit pricey at about 20 times earnings, strong demand for data storage, combined with the EMC's solid market position, meant that it should grow at a pretty rapid clip. So I bought a pretty good-sized position for my piddling portfolio.

I then watched the stock go from $5 to $100 in three years—and right back to $5 a year later. I sold about a third of my position at a pretty high price, but I watched the majority come right back down again. I had made a great purchase decision, but my overall return on the investment would have been far, far better had I been smarter about selling.

Ask any professional investor what he or she thinks is the hardest part of investing, and most will tell you that knowing when to sell ranks up there near the top—if not right at the top. In this chapter, I want to give you a road map for selling well, because selling a stock at the right time, and for the right reasons, is just as important to your investment returns as buying a stock with a lot of upside potential.

Sell for the Right Reasons

Ask yourself these questions the next time you think about selling, and if you can't answer yes to one or more, don't sell.

- Did I make a mistake?
- Has the company changed for the worse?
- Is there a better place for my money?
- Has the stock become too large a portion of my portfolio?

Perhaps the most painful reason to sell is that you were simply wrong. But if you missed something significant when you first analyzed the company—whatever it was— then your original investment thesis may very well not hold water. Maybe you thought management would be able to turn around or sell a money-losing division, but instead the company decided to plow more money into that segment. Perhaps you thought the company had a strong competitive advantage, but then the competition started eating its lunch; or maybe you overestimated the success of a new product. No matter what the mistake was, it's rarely worth hanging on to a stock that you bought for a reason that is no longer valid. Cut your losses and move on.

I did just this many years ago with a company that manufactured commercial movie projectors. The company had strong market share and a good track record, and multiscreen theaters were springing up like weeds across the country. Unfortunately, my growth expectations turned out to be way too high, because the multiplex-building boom was waning. Theater owners started to get into financial trouble, and they were a lot more worried about paying their bills—especially the interest on their debt—than they were in building new theaters. I was down quite a bit on the investment by the time I figured this out, but I sold anyway. Good thing I did, too, because the shares subsequently plunged to penny-stock territory.

I should note that this is far easier said than done, because we tend to anchor on the price at which we bought a stock, and we hate losing money. (In fact, numerous psychological studies have proved that people experience almost twice as much pain when they lose money than they experience pleasure when they gain the exact same amount.) This behavior causes us to focus on irrelevant information—the price at which we purchased a stock, which has zero effect on the company's future prospects—instead of much more relevant information, such as the fact that our original assessment of the company's future may have been flat-out wrong.

One trick you can use to avoid anchoring is this: Each time you buy a stock, write down why you bought it and roughly what you expect to happen with the company's financial results. I'm not talking about quarterly earnings forecasts, just rough expectations: Do you expect sales growth to be steady or to accelerate? Do you expect profit margins to go up or down? Then, if the company takes a turn for the worse, pull out your piece of paper and see whether your reasons for buying the stock still make sense. If they do, hold on or buy more. But if they don't, selling is likely your best option—*regardless of whether you've made or lost money on the shares.*

The second reason to sell is if a company's fundamentals deteriorate substantially and don't look like they're going to rebound. For a long-term investor, this is likely to be one of the more common reasons to sell: Even the best companies can hit a wall after years of success. You may very well have been 100 percent right in your initial assessment of the company's prospects, its valuation, and its competitive advantages, and you may have had a lot of success owning the stock—but as economist John Maynard Keynes once said, "When the facts change, I change my mind."

Here's a recent example from a company I once covered for Morningstar: Getty Images. This is a fascinating company that capitalized on photography's digital migration by building a massive database of digital images that it distributes to ad agencies and other large image consumers. Getty essentially became the industry's largest marketplace for images, making it easy for photographers to upload images to its database, and for image users to find exactly the image they need. For a time it was a great business, with strong growth rates, high returns on capital, and massive operating leverage.

So what happened? Essentially, the same digital technology that built the company made it less relevant. As high-quality digital imaging became more accessible to a wider range of users, it became easier to create professional-quality images with cheaper cameras. This led to the rise of web sites selling images that were admittedly lower-quality than the average Getty image, but that were much cheaper (a few dollars versus a few hundred dollars), and good enough for less demanding users. Couple this with the fact that online images don't need to be of as high quality as ones used in print media, and Getty's economics and growth prospects changed markedly for the worse.

The third reason to sell is that you come across a better place for your money. As an investor with limited capital, you want to always be sure that your investments have the highest possible expected return. So, selling a modestly undervalued stock to fund the purchase of a ridiculously mouth-watering opportunity is perfectly logical—and a darned good idea. Of course, taxes come into play here, and you may need a larger difference in potential upside to justify a sale in a taxable account than in a tax-qualified one, but it is nonetheless something to keep in mind. I wouldn't recommend constant portfolio tweaking to move from stocks with 20 percent upside to stocks with 30 percent upside, but when a great opportunity comes along, sometimes you need to sell an existing stock to fund the idea.

For example, when the market sold off during the credit crunch in late summer of 2007, financial services stocks were absolutely crushed. Some were deservedly so, but as is usually the case, Wall Street threw a lot of babies out with the bathwater, and many stocks were whacked down to ridiculously cheap levels. Now, I normally keep at least 5 to 10 percent of my personal account in cash so that I have dry powder for occasions just like this one—you never know when the market will lose its mind—but for a number of reasons, I was caught with very little spare cash during this particular sell-off. So, I started comparing the potential upside from my existing positions with some of the financial stocks that Wall Street was putting on sale. The net result was that I sold a position that I hadn't owned for very long, but which had only modest upside potential, to fund the purchase of a bank trading at below book value, which had already agreed to be taken over at a higher price—a very worthwhile trade-off.

Remember that sometimes the better place for your money may very well be cash. If a stock has far surpassed what you think it is worth and your expected return from now on is actually negative, then selling it makes sense even if you don't have any other good investment ideas at the time. After all, even the modest return that cash delivers is better than a negative return—which is exactly what you'll get if you own a stock that has run beyond even the most optimistic assessment of its value.

The final reason to sell is the best one of all. If you've had a screaming success with an investment and its market value has grown to make up a big chunk of your portfolio, it may make sense to dial down the risk and shrink the position. This is a very personal decision, as some people are very comfortable with concentrated portfolios (at one point in early 2007, half my personal portfolio was in just two stocks), but many investors are more comfortable limiting individual positions to 5 percent or so of their portfolios. It's your call, but if you get the willies having 10 percent of your portfolio in a single stock, even if it still looks undervalued, listen to your stomach and trim the position. You have to live with your own portfolio, after all, and if keeping position sizes down makes you more comfortable, so be it.

Before closing this chapter, I want to quickly draw your attention to the fact that none of the four reasons to sell that I've laid out is based on what happens to stock prices. They're all centered on what happens, or is likely to happen, to the *values* of the companies whose stock you own. Selling just because a stock price has dropped makes absolutely no sense whatsoever, unless the value of the business has declined as well. Conversely, selling just because a stock has skyrocketed makes no sense, unless the value of the business has not increased in tandem.

It's very tempting to use the past performance of the stocks in your portfolio to decide when to sell. Remember, though, that what matters is how you expect a business to perform in the future, not how its share price has performed in the past. There's no reason why stocks that are up a lot should drop, just as there's no reason why stocks that have cratered have to come back eventually. If you own a stock that is down 20 percent and the business has gotten worse and isn't getting better, you might as well book the loss and take the tax break. The trick is to always stay focused on the future performance of the business, not the past performance of the shares.

The Bottom Line

1. If you have made a mistake analyzing the company, and your original reason for buying is no longer valid, selling is likely to be your best option.

2. It would be great if solid companies never changed, but that's rarely the case. If the fundamentals of a company change permanently—not temporarily—for the worse, you may want to sell.

3. The best investors are always looking for the best places for their money. Selling a modestly undervalued stock to fund the purchase of a supercheap stock is a smart strategy. So is selling an overvalued stock and parking the proceeds in cash if there aren't any attractively priced stocks at the time.

4. Selling a stock when it becomes a huge part of your portfolio can make sense, depending on your risk tolerance.

Conclusion

More than Numbers

I LOVE THE STOCK MARKET.

I don't love all the raving and ranting about job reports and Federal Reserve meetings, nor the breathless discussions of quarterly earnings reports minutes after they hit the newswires. Most if this is just noise, anyway, and has little bearing on the long-term value of individual companies. I largely ignore it, and so should you.

What does get me up in the morning is the opportunity to see how thousands of companies all try to solve the exact same problem: How do I make more money than my competitor across the street? Companies can create competitive advantages in a wide variety of ways, and seeing what separates the great from the merely good is an endlessly fascinating intellectual exercise.

Of course, it can be financially rewarding as well, assuming you wait patiently for quality businesses to trade for less than their intrinsic value before making an investment. The key is to realize that you can let the companies in your portfolio do some of the heavy lifting for you in terms of investment returns. Companies with strong competitive advantages can regularly post returns on capital of 20+ percent, which is a rate of return that very few money managers can achieve over long periods of time.* The opportunity to become part owner of enterprises that can compound capital at such a rate—especially if your ownership stakes are purchased for 80 cents on the dollar—has the potential to build a lot of wealth over time.

One thing many people don't realize about investing is that it's not just a numbers game. You do need to understand some basic accounting to get the most out of financial statements, but I've known some pretty smart accountants who weren't much good at analyzing businesses or picking stocks. Understanding how cash flows through a company,

---

*As of mid-2007, exactly 24 nonsector funds out of more than 5,550 in Morningstar's database had managed to generate annualized returns above 15 percent over the past 15 years—not an easy task.

and how that process is reflected in the financial statements, is necessary, but by no means sufficient.

To be a truly good investor, you need to read widely. The major business press—the *Wall Street Journal, Fortune, Barron's*—is a good start, because it helps you to expand your mental database of companies. The more companies you are familiar with, the easier it will be to make comparisons, find patterns, and see themes that strengthen or weaken competitive advantages. I would argue strongly that reading about companies will add infinitely more value to your investment process than will reading about short-term market movements, macroeconomic trends, or interest-rate forecasts. One annual report is worth 10 speeches by a Federal Reserve chairman.

Once you've made these publications part of your investment diet, move on to books about—and by—successful money managers. There's no substitute for learning about investing from people 'who have practiced it successfully, after all. Quarterly shareholder letters are valuable for the same reason, and they have the added benefit of being free. In my opinion, the quarterly letters written by solid money managers about their portfolios are some of the most underused investment resources on the planet—and given the price, they are certainly worth more than you're paying for them.

Finally, there is a burgeoning literature about how people make investment decisions, and why that process is often filled with hidden biases. Books like *Why Smart People Make Big Money Mistakes—and How to Correct Them* by Gary Belsky and Thomas Gilovich (Simon & Schuster, 1999); *The Halo Effect* by Phil Rosenzweig (Simon & Schuster, 2007); and *Your Money and Your Brain* by Jason Zweig (Simon & Schuster, 2007) will help you see the flaws in your own decision-making process, and will help you make smarter decisions about your investments.

I hope that the ideas in this book will do the same.